SUCCESSFUL MOVES FROM THE OPENING TO THE ENDGAME

WINNING GO

RICHARD BOZULICH and PETER SHOTWELL

T0162926

TUTTLE PUBLISHING
Tokyo • Rutland, Vermont • Singapore

Published by Tuttle Publishing, an imprint of Periplus Editions (HK) Ltd.

www.tuttlepublishing.com

Library of Congress Cataloging-in-Publication Data

Shotwell, Peter, 1941-
  Winning go : successful moves from the opening to the endgame / Peter Shotwell and Richard Bozulich.
    p. cm.
  ISBN 978-4-8053-1072-4 (pbk.)
  1. Go (Game) I. Bozulich, Richard, 1936- II. Title.
  GV1459.5.S58 2010
  794'.4--dc22

                          2010005712

ISBN 978-4-8053-1072-4

Distributed by

North America, Latin America & Europe
Tuttle Publishing
364 Innovation Drive
North Clarendon, VT 05759-9436 U.S.A.
Tel: 1 (802) 773-8930
Fax: 1 (802) 773-6993
info@tuttlepublishing.com
www.tuttlepublishing.com

Japan
Tuttle Publishing
Yaekari Building, 3rd Floor
5-4-12 Osaki
Shinagawa-ku
Tokyo 141 0032
Tel: (81) 3 5437-0171
Fax: (81) 3 5437-0755
tuttle-sales@gol.com

Asia Pacific
Berkeley Books Pte. Ltd.
61 Tai Seng Avenue #02-12
Singapore 534167
Tel: (65) 6280-1330
Fax: (65) 6280-6290
inquiries@periplus.com.sg
www.periplus.com

14 13 12 11 10   6 5 4 3 2 1

Printed in Singapore

TUTTLE PUBLISHING® is a registered trademark of Tuttle Publishing, a division of Periplus Editions (HK) Ltd.

CONTENTS

Acknowledgements

We would like to thank Bud Sperry, our patient and understanding editor, along with the Anthoney Chua and Alphone Tea and others at Tuttle who saw things through some rough spots in the production.

And thanks to Anders Kierulf, whose Smart Go program enabled the diagrams to be produced as .eps files from their original .sgf format. His program also has many other useful features and can be seen and purchased at www.smartgo.com.

Thanks also to our agent, Jim Fitzgerald, who suggested the book.

And, as always, thanks to members of the American Go Association and the Nihon Kiin in Japan for all of their support in spreading go throughout the world and making possible books such as this one and others from Tuttle and Kiseido Publications.

— *Richard Bozulich & Peter Shotwell*

CHAPTER ONE

Katachi—Making Good Shape

Unlike chess, the underlying basis of go is the mysterious necessity for making good shapes and avoiding bad ones. As this book will demonstrate, in all phases of the game, good shapes are resilient to attack because they are working efficiently, while poor ones are vulnerable and subject to harassment. Spotting the differences and knowing what to do about them is the primary key for rapid improvement in playing ability.

Short Summary of the Fundamentals of Good and Bad Shapes

Efficient Expansions

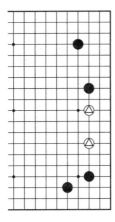

Diagram 1

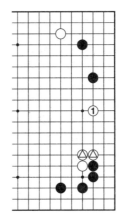

Diagram 2

The two marked white stones on the second line in Diagram 1 are separated by two spaces. This is an efficient extension because these stones cannot be split and have sufficient resiliency to live.

From a wall of two stones (the marked ones in Diagram 2), extending three spaces with 1 is also a good extension. It makes efficient use of the two-stone wall.

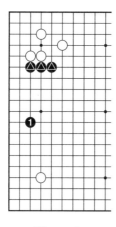

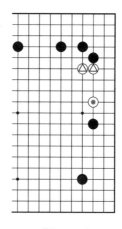

| Diagram 3 | Diagram 4 |

From a wall such as the three marked stones in Diagram 3, a four-space extension would also be a good move.

There are times when only a two-space extension can be made from a two stone wall. The extension in Diagram 4 is a bit narrow, but what it lacks in efficiency, it makes up for in strength.

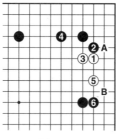

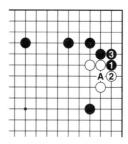

| Diagram 5 | Diagram 6 |

Moreover, in high-handicap games, there are times when only a one-space extension is possible from a two-stone wall. White's position is quite cramped, but at least there is potential to make eye shape with a move such as 5. If Black *A*, White can expand with *B*; if Black *B*, White *A*.

After White 5 in Diagram 5, Black might secure the corner with 1 and 3 in Diagram 6, but White makes good shape with 2. This is good shape because White has almost made an eye around the point *A* and has room to move into the center.

Making Good Shape

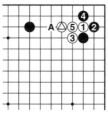

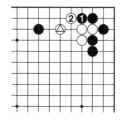

Diagram 7   Diagram 8

White 1 and 3 in Diagram 7 are standard moves. However, when Black puts White into *atari* ("ah-tar-ee") and threatens to capture, White 5 forms the classic bad shape commonly known as an "empty triangle." However, if the marked stone was at A, this would be a reasonable result for White. For example, in Diagram 8, if the marked stone was in place and Black pushed in with 1, a good shape like the one in Diagram 6 on the other side of the board would result.

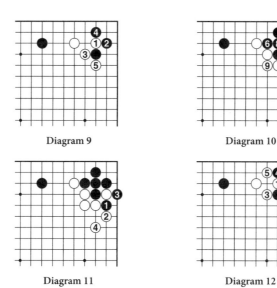

Diagram 9   Diagram 10

Diagram 11   Diagram 12

White should answer Black 4 in Diagram 7 with the atari of 5 in Diagram 9. Black will capture with 6 in Diagram 10, White ataries again with 7 and Black has to "connect" with 8. White can then connect on the outside with 9. Later, Black will have to capture a stone with 1 and 3 in Diagram 11, but White can make good shape with 2 and 4.

Instead of 5 in Diagram 9, White could answer Black 4 by falling back to 5 in Diagram 12. But this is a special technique when Black's stones are too strong in this area and White is prepared to fight a *ko* ("koh") to make a living group. This is explained on the next page.

Ponnuki and Ko

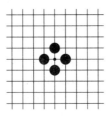

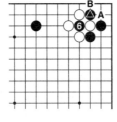

Diagram 13   Diagram 14

After a capture, a *ponnuki* ("pon-new-key") shape can radiate influence all over the board. Since the shape of the white stones in Diagram 12 was almost a ponnuki, White 5 made good shape.

If Black takes with 6, since no position can be repeated in go, White can make a move elsewhere that threatens Black with a bigger loss. If Black responds, it is the beginning of a "two-step" ko and White can take back. This back-and-forth can continue for many moves with the size of the ko "threats" diminishing, but if White has calculated correctly, conceding two smaller loses and capturing the marked stone with *A* and *B* results in a living, impregnable position in the corner.

The Mouth Shape

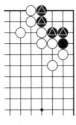

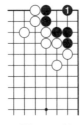

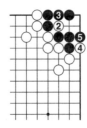

Diagram 15   Diagram 16   Diagram 17

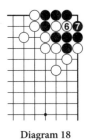

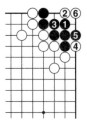

Diagram 18   Diagram 19

The marked stones in Diagram 15 are called the "mouth shape". However, in this case, the shape is incomplete and Black needs another move to secure life. Black can do this by putting a "tooth" on the vital point of this shape with 1 in Diagram 16. Black's stones are now absolutely secure. If White tried to kill the black group with an atari at 2 in Diagram 17, Black could defend with 3 and White's subsequent moves in Diagram 18 would be futile.

Any other reinforcing move will fail. For example, Black cannot live with 1 in Diagram 19 because White would attack with the "placement" of 2. If Black connects with 3 to prevent the two stones on the left from being captured, White can play 4 and 6, leaving the black group with only one eye.

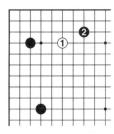

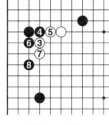

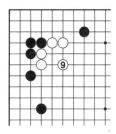

Diagram 20   Diagram 21   Diagram 22

Here is an example of how the mouth shape can occur in a game. The exchange of White 1 for Black 2 in Diagram 20 is the start of a local skirmish called a *joseki* ("joe-se-key") in which both sides are satisfied in terms of profit and/or influence. The moves from White 3 to Black 8 in Diagram 21 unfold naturally, and White has made the mouth shape with 7. It is now urgent that White secures this shape by playing on the vital point with 9 in Diagram 22. Getting a second eye at the top or even in the center will be easy.

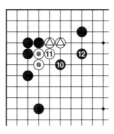

Diagram 23

If White plays 9 elsewhere, Black will attack White with 10 in Diagram 23, aiming to split up the group of stones by cutting at 11. If White defends there, Black will jump to 12, and the white stones are under attack.

The white stones in Diagram 23 are a perfect example of bad shape. They are not working efficiently in that they have two empty triangles (the two circled stones and two triangled stones combined with 11). Moreover, they have no eye-making potential in the center. A beginner might feel desperate and try to make one eye at the top and then escape into the center, but there is a better way to play ...

Heavy Stones

The clump of white stones in Diagram 23 are "heavy" and trying to rescue them would not be a good idea. A better strategy is to abandon them for the moment and play elsewhere. Their loss might look big, but a strong Black player would gain even more profit by solidifying territory and gaining influence while chasing them.

Also, there may be a way to rescue them as the game develops and the fighting spills into the upper-left.

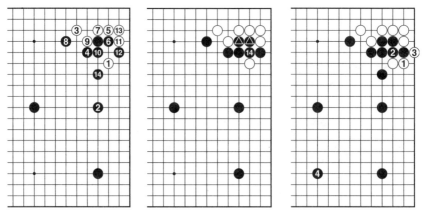

Diagram 24   Diagram 25   Diagram 26

Another example of how a less-than-useful clump of stones can develop is from the beginning of this five-stone handicap game. After White plays 1 in Diagram 24 , the pincer of Black 2 is the perfect strategic point. The correct response to White 13 is Black 14. This is the joseki move, meaning that both sides will be satisfied at the end of the sequence if it is played correctly.

However, a common mistake that amateurs make is to connect with 14 in Diagram 25. This move certainly stops White from linking up to the right side with the moves of 1 and 3 in Diagram 26. However, White would lose the initiative by doing this and Black would get to take another strategic point with 4 at the bottom. Either way, Black would be amassing overwhelming influence in the center and, by connecting with 14 in Diagram 25, the two marked stones are not working to take territory nor are they projecting any strategic influence.

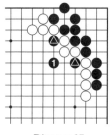

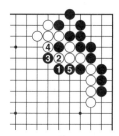

Diagram 27   Diagram 28

In Diagram 27, Black has taken about 20 points of territory in the corner. White's central influence seems to provide sufficient compensation, but the shape is defective. Black can jump ahead of the two marked stones with 1 in Diagram 27, threatening to capture them. If White escapes by capturing with 2 and 4 in Diagram 28, Black "squeezes" with 5 ...

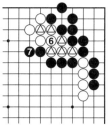

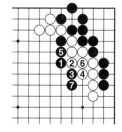

Diagram 29   Diagram 30

... and White connects with 6 in Diagram 29. However, the stones at the top are useless and Black finishes off the sequence by extending to 7. If White plays 2 and 4 in the other direction, as in Diagram 30, the result is the same after White 6.

It would have been better to repair the shape at first or, if the mistake has been made, to play elsewhere and hope to come back to threaten on the outside and force Black to capture while keeping the initiative.

Playing Lightly by Making Sabaki

Playing "lightly" is the opposite of playing "heavily," so the technique of *sabaki* ("sa-bak-kee") is used to sacrifice some of the stones in order that the others may live. This is the correct strategy when a group of stones is outnumbered in one part of the board and the aim is not to make territory. Instead, good shape, rich in eye potential, is needed so that, if attacked, two eyes or an escape into the center can be made.

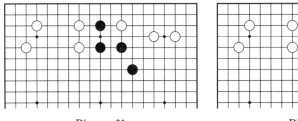

Diagram 31   Diagram 32

The black stones in Diagram 31 do not have eye shape, while the white stones on the left and right are strong. However, if Black starts at 1, White *hanes* ("hannays") with 2, Black cuts with 3, White 4 ataries and Black descends to 5 to sacrifice two stones.

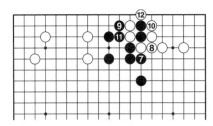

Diagram 33   Diagram 34

After White 6, Black forces with 7, then makes White capture two stones by playing 9 and 11. Black ends with a completed mouth shape and the initiative to make the next move. Moreover, the group is firmly out into the center and will have no problem getting two eyes.

A mouth shape also results from Black 1 and 3 in Diagram 34, but White will then be able to play elsewhere.

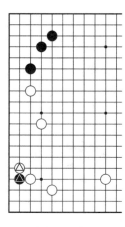

Diagram 35

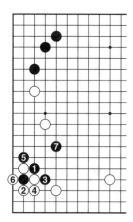

Diagram 36

In Diagram 35, White has mapped out a framework of territory in the lower-left. Black begins an invasion by exchanging the marked stones and now Black must find a way to make sabaki.

Cutting with 1 in Diagram 36 is the natural move. If White goes after the invading stone with 2, Black can force White to capture with 3 and 5. Black can now jump into the center with 7, a typical example of a light move.

Thickness and Thinness

Related to the subjects of the two previous sections, a "thick" position is one that either has eyes or no places where a "cut" can be made to separate and weaken the group. Therefore, these positions are useful for attack because they are not vulnerable.

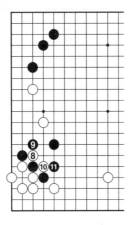

Diagram 37

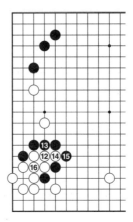

Diagram 38

Consider, for example, what happens if White keeps going with a cut at 8 in Diagram 37 and continues on as in Diagram 38. Black ends with a thick wall that radiates influence throughout the board and especially onto the now thin and vulnerable white stones on the left side.

In the chapters that follow, the making of good shapes and the destruction of bad ones will be demonstrated in all phases of the game of go.

CHAPTER TWO

Fuseki—The Opening

The opening, or *fuseki* ("foo-se-key") as it is called in Japanese, is where the groundwork for strategies is laid out. There are a number of principles that all go players must learn if they are going to master this phase of the game. This is not a complete list, but it contains the most important ones.

Secure stones so that they don't come under attack

Weak stones are a burden, since they can come under attack. The point of attacking a weak group is not necessarily to kill it (although this is usually the underlying threat), but to harass it in order to make territory or build influence. Securing stones is usually the first priority in the opening, even before making important extensions.

Attack the opponent's weak stones

Weak stones often lack eye shape, so when they are attacked, if sabaki is not used, they usually must escape into the center. In the process, they will get almost no territory, but the attacker can take profit by making territory and/or influence.

Expand territorial frameworks at the expense of the opponent's framework

When both players have competing frameworks of territory, the player who first plays at the point of mutual expansion will gain a great advantage.

Keep opponents confined to a low position

Pressing down from above and confining the opponent to the second or third line results in gaining outside influence that will ultimately result in territory.

Keep stones linked up and don't allow them to become isolated and split up

When stones become separated there is a danger that one group of them will find itself struggling to make life. In the meantime, the opponent will be building influence while the weak group ends up with just a few points of territory.

Don't approach thickness

When the opponent has a thick position that is strong and invulnerable to attack, it is not a good idea to play a stone too close to it. There are a number of corollaries to this principle. Two examples are to "Use thickness to attack" and "Try not to use thickness to make territory."

Often it is best to play where the other side would like to play

This is a vast and general thought that permeates all go playing, particularly when it makes the difference between gaining or losing territory and having good or bad shape.

Opening Problems
Black to Play

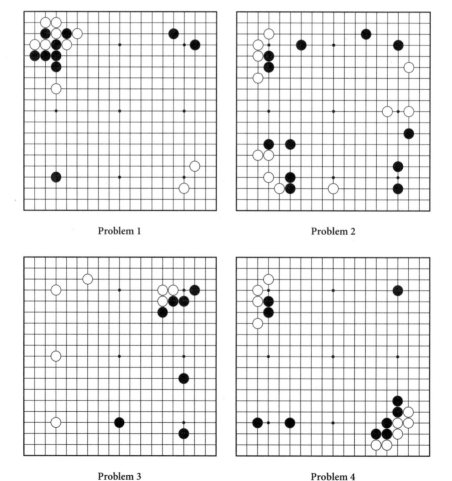

Problem 1   Problem 2

Problem 3   Problem 4

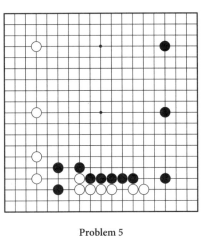

Problem 5

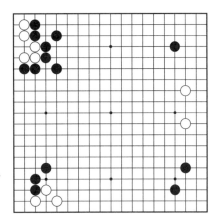

Problem 6

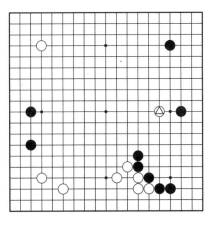

Problem 7

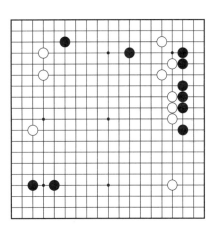

Problem 8

Problem 9

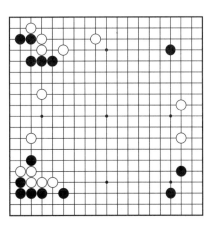

Problem 10

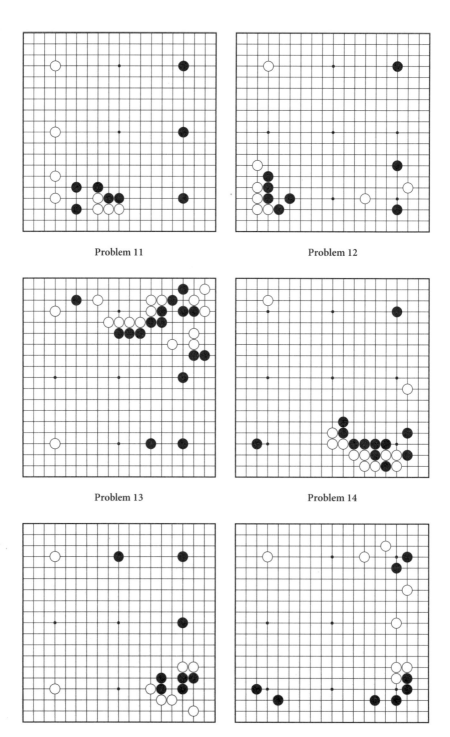

Problem 11

Problem 12

Problem 13

Problem 14

Problem 15

Problem 16

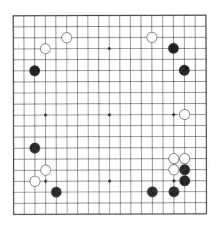

Problem 17

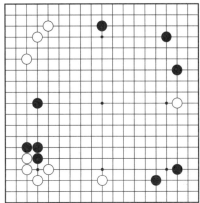

Problem 18

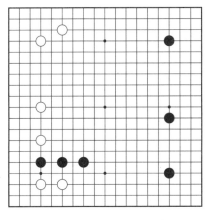

Problem 19

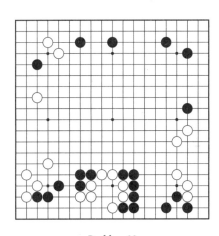

Problem 20

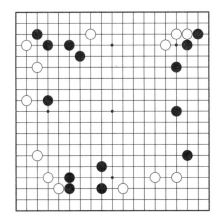

Problem 21

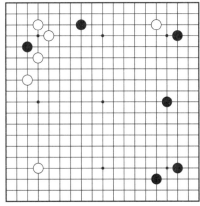

Problem 22

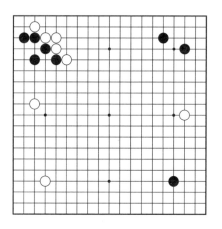

Problem 23

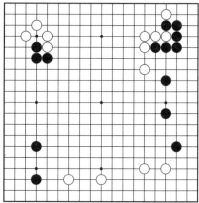

Problem 24

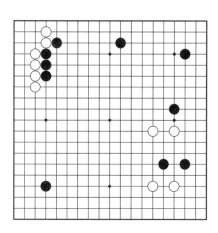

Problem 25

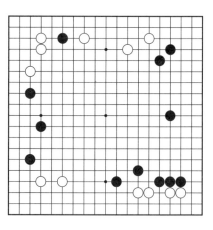

Problem 26

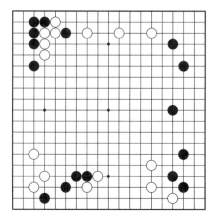

Problem 27

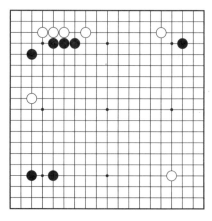

Problem 28

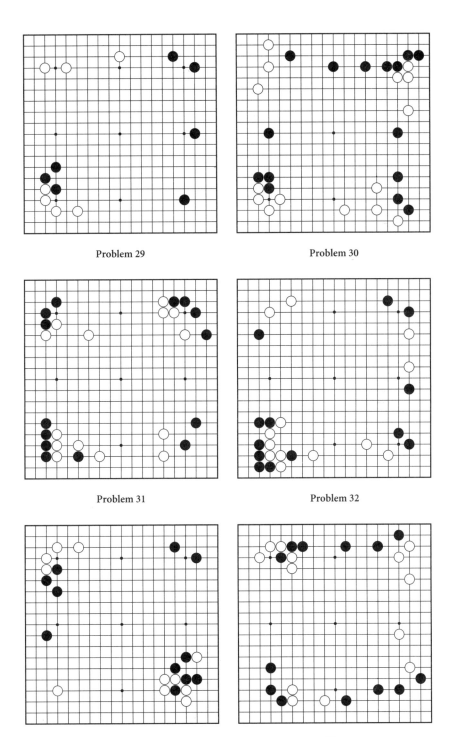

Problem 29

Problem 30

Problem 31

Problem 32

Problem 33

Problem 34

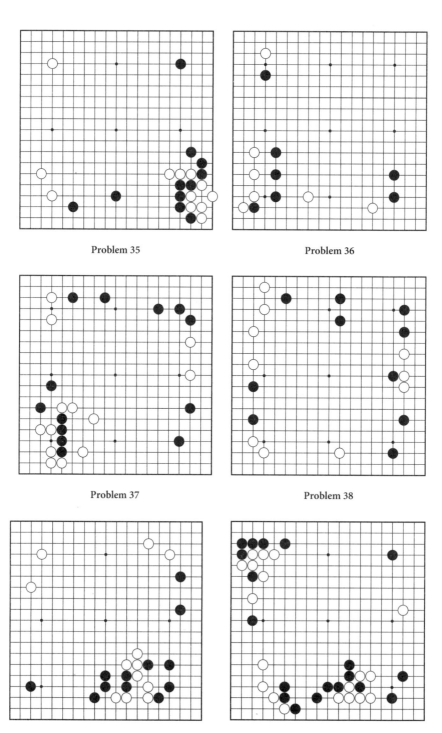

Problem 35

Problem 36

Problem 37

Problem 38

Problem 39

Problem 40

Answers to the Opening Problems

Problem 1

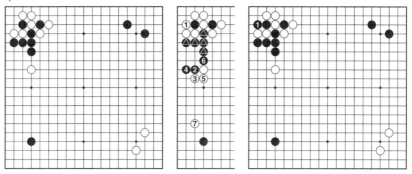

Correct Answer

Capturing two white stones with Black 1 follows the principle of securing stones so that they don't come under attack.

If Black lets White capture with 1 in the small diagram, the marked stones don't have two eyes. If Black tries to make those eyes with 2 to 6, White gains influence on the left side and can approach the black stone in the lower-left with 7, mapping out territory.

Problem 2

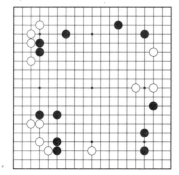 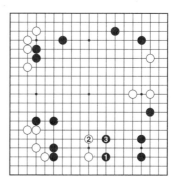

Correct Answer

Attacking the lone white stone by extending to Black 1 follows the principle of attacking weak stones. White's stone has no room to maneuver because Black is strong on the left. All it can do is to try to escape into the center, a move that will not gain any territory. On the other hand, by extending from the corner enclosure, Black has mapped out territory on the right. If White escapes by jumping to 3, Black can keep up the pressure with 2, reinforcing the territory on the right.

Problem 3

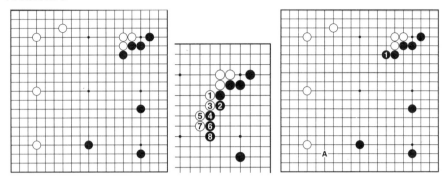

Correct Answer

By extending to 1, Black expands a large territorial framework while reducing White's.

If Black were to play elsewhere, for example, with an approach at *A*, White's framework would expand with 1 to 7 in the small diagram. Forced to answer, Black would lose the initiative and end up compressed along the side.

Problem 4

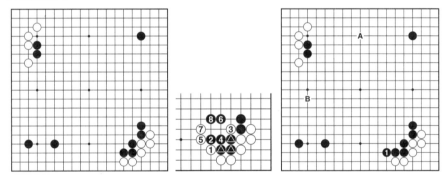

Correct Answer

Black 1 follows the principle of keeping the opponent confined to the second line. This move also increases Black's influence towards the center.

If Black were to play at *A* or *B* instead, White would play at 1 and break out of the bottom. Black's marked stones are short of "liberties", so White could force the sequence to 7 in the small diagram.

Problem 5

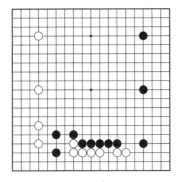
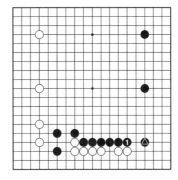

Correct Answer

Black 1 is an urgent move that "links up" Black's stones on the left to the marked stone in the corner. Together with the stone in the middle of the right side, Black now has a magnificent framework of territory that radiates influence throughout the board.

If White were allowed to play at 1, the marked black stone would be isolated and Black would no longer have a coherent strategy.

Problem 6

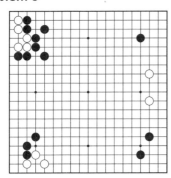
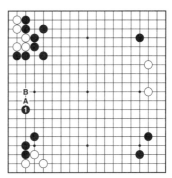

Correct Answer

The principle to follow here is, "Don't approach thickness." Black needs to reinforce the three stones below, but the white stones in the upper-left are thick and strong, so Black should not approach them too closely. Black 1 is the perfect distance.

Extending as far as A or B would leave Black's position open to an invasion. In that case, the stones below and the stone at A or B would be separated and could run into trouble. This would not happen immediately, but it is a possibility that would be a nagging concern to Black throughout the game. Go players would say that there would be "bad" *aji* ("ah-gee"), which, in Japanese, literally means it would leave a "bad taste."

Problem 7

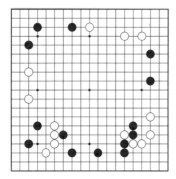 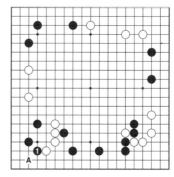

Correct Answer

Black 1 is a huge move. Not only does it take the territory in the corner, but it also prevents the four white stones from making eye shape. Once Black makes this move, White's stones will have to run out into the center and try to get two eyes so Black would be able to harass them while gaining territory and influence.

If Black omitted this move and White was allowed to slide to *A*, the situation would be reversed. White would have no trouble making two eyes in the corner, while the two black stones would be deprived of their "base" and would need to escape.

Problem 8

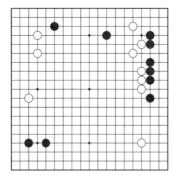 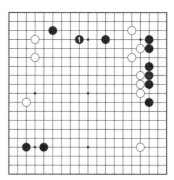

Correct Answer

Black's two stones at the top are spread out too thinly. White has a thick wall on the right and a strong position on the left, so Black has to reinforce these stones with 1 and claim the territory there as well.

If Black omits playing 1, White will take this point and the black stones at the top would be in trouble.

Problem 9

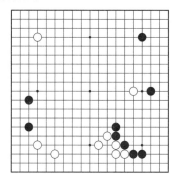 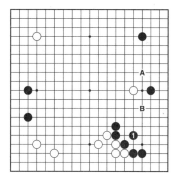

Correct Answer

Against the cap of the marked stone, answering with a "knight's move" at *A* or *B* is usually the proper response. However, in this case, it is urgent that Black defend the two cutting points at the bottom by making shape with the diagonal connection of 1.

Problem 10

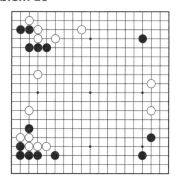 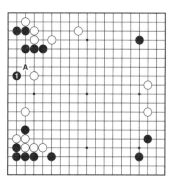

Correct Answer

Black's stones do not have eye shape, so Black must slide to 1 to secure them. After this move, White can no longer make much territory on the left side.

If Black omits this move, White will attack the five black stones with *A* and map out some territory besides. Black must escape with no territory while White's would be enlarged and solidified.

Problem 11

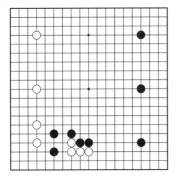
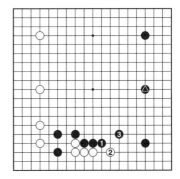

Correct Answer

Black 1 forces White to crawl submissively along the third line. White tries to get ahead of Black by jumping to 2, but Black stays ahead with the knight's move of 3. Black's wall radiates influence throughout the board, and the marked stone is perfectly placed to make a huge territorial framework on the right side.

Problem 12

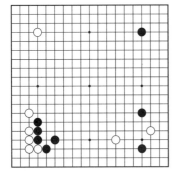
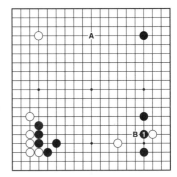

Correct Answer

It is urgent that Black "attach" with 1. This move not only links up the two stones in the lower-right, it also separates White's two stones.

Instead of 1, Black A is certainly a big move, but if White answered with B, the black stones would face an uphill battle after being separated.

Problem 13

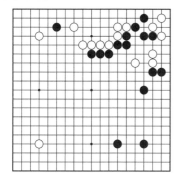 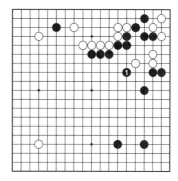

Correct Answer

Black 1 "blocks" the escape route of white stones in the corner, threatening to kill them. It also makes a huge territorial framework on the right side. Now, White has to passively make two eyes, giving Black another strategic move on the outside.

Problem 14

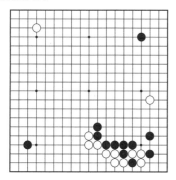 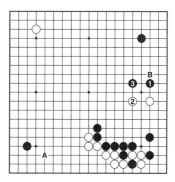

Correct Answer

Black's stones are thick at the bottom and should be used to attack the lone white stone on the right side with 1. If White runs into the center with 2, Black chases with 3, mapping out territory in the upper-right. In contrast, White's territorial gain is zero.

Instead of 1, making a corner enclosure with Black *A* is also a big move, but White would then extend to *B*, securing a safe position on the right side. Black's thick wall would go to waste.

Problem 15

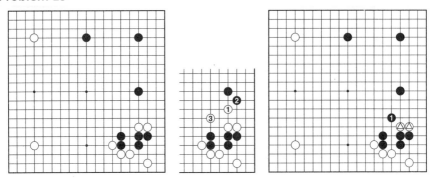

Correct Answer

Black must take control of the two marked stones and the territory there by playing 1.

If Black omits this move and plays elsewhere, White will play 1 in the small diagram. If Black 2, White will jump out to 3 and the black group below has to run for its life.

Problem 16

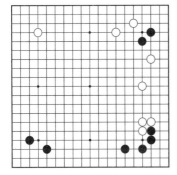 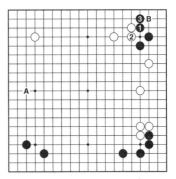

Correct Answer

Black's two stones in the upper-right corner do not have a secure base so one must be made by attaching with 1, then descending to 3. They are now safe.

If Black neglects playing 1 and extends to A, (which is a good point locally), White would slide to B and the two black stones would be under attack between two strong White positions.

Problem 17

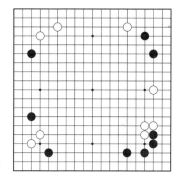 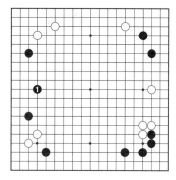

Correct Answer

Black's two stones on the left are spread out too thinly and need to be reinforced. Black 1 on the fourth line accomplishes this and it strikes a perfect balance with the two allies on the third line.

If Black plays elsewhere, White will invade somewhere around this point, and Black's position on the left would crumble.

Problem 18

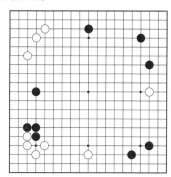 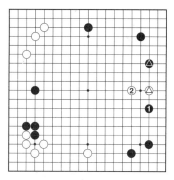

Correct Answer

Black should extend to 1. By squeezing the marked white stone against the marked black one, it extends the enclosure at the bottom and makes it safer. While Black is mapping out territory, White is under pressure and must jump to 2, which gains nothing.

Problem 19

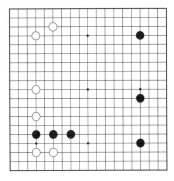 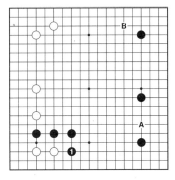

Correct Answer

Black should jump down to 1, threatening to kill the white stones in the lower left corner while building a vast territorial framework on the right. If White defends in the corner, Black can reinforce the framework by making a corner enclosure with *A*.

If Black plays at *A* or *B* instead of 1, White will seek security by playing at 1. This would also destroy Black's framework at the bottom.

Problem 20

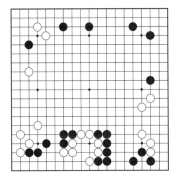 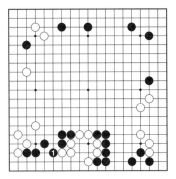

Correct Answer

In this position, 1 is the vital point for both sides. For Black, it means the group is safe.

If White were to play there, the black group would be just a string of stones without a base and could easily die under a strong assault.

Problem 21

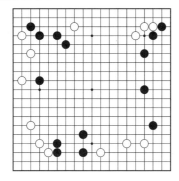 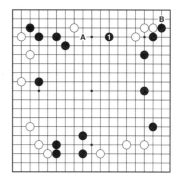

Correct Answer

White's stones at the top are spread out too thinly, so Black should invade with 1.

If White responds by running away with *A*, Black will attack the three white stones on the right by descending to *B*. If White defends instead, Black will take control of the top left by blocking at *A*.

Problem 22

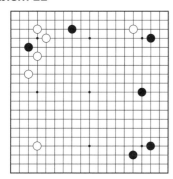 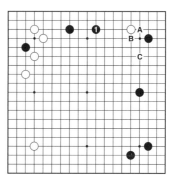

Correct Answer

Black must secure the stone at the top by extending to 1.

It is tempting for Black to exchange Black *A* for White *B*, then secure the upper right side with the knight's move of *C*, but this would enable White to make a "pincer" on the key point of 1. With the strong white wall on the left, the lone black stones at the top would have a difficult struggle to survive.

Problem 23

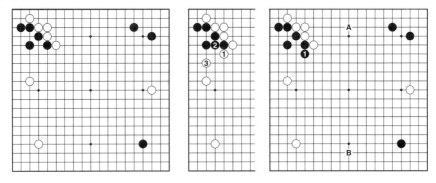

Correct Answer

Extending to Black 1 is mandatory. This move gives the black stones good shape and makes them invulnerable to attacks. They also exert an influence on White's thin position on the left and have an influence on the five white stones in the top left.

If Black neglects to play this move and plays an extension at *A* or *B*, White will atari with 1 and then confine Black's stones to the corner with 3 in the middle diagram.

Problem 24

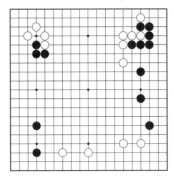
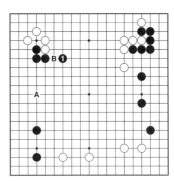

Correct Answer

White would like to make a big framework at the top, so Black must neutralize this area by jumping to 1. This also expands Black's influence on the left side.

Reinforcing the left side with a move such as Black *A* would be passive. White would respond with *B* and expand the top framework.

Problem 25

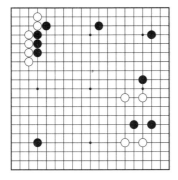 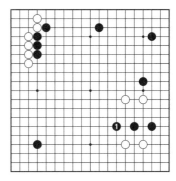

Correct Answer

The two principles that apply here are, "Don't allow stones to be confined so that they have to struggle to live," and "Split the opponent's stones." Therefore, Black must jump out into the center with 1. This move keeps the white stones separated and also prevents White from playing at 1, a move that would confine Black's stones to the right side. If that happened, Black's struggles to live would adversely affect the framework at the top while strengthening White's positions on the outside.

Problem 26

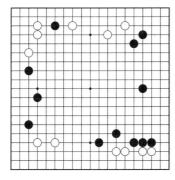 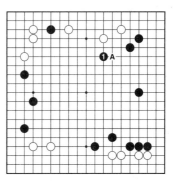

Correct Answer

Black builds a large framework with 1. This also keeps White from expanding at A to threaten the Black's upper-right territory.

Problem 27

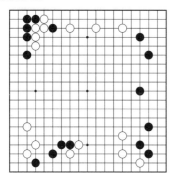 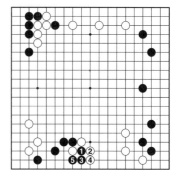

Correct Answer

Black should secure the position in the lower- left by cutting with 1 and following through with 3 and 5. White stakes out territory in the lower-right with 2 and 4, but the security of Black's position takes priority.

Problem 28

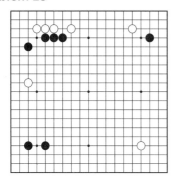 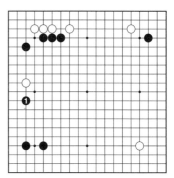

Correct Answer

Black's thick wall in the upper-left should be used to attack the lone white stone with 1. With the ideal extension from Black's corner enclosure at the bottom, this also stakes out future territory.

Problem 29

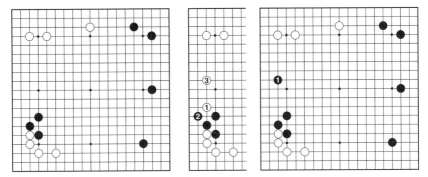

Correct Answer

Black has to secure the three stones in the lower-left by extending to 1.

If Black omits this move, White will attack with 1, as in the small diagram. After Black 2 and White 3, Black's four stones would be "floating" without a base.

Problem 30

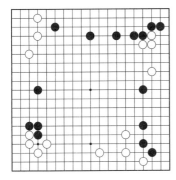 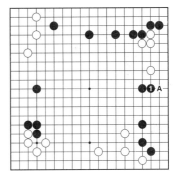

Correct Answer

Black should make a two-stone "iron pillar" with 1. This move secures the territory in the lower-right and, at the same time, attacks the four white stones above.

If Black omits this move, White's slide to A would secure the group and destroy Black's territory in the lower-right.

Problem 31

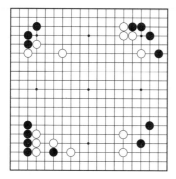 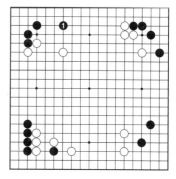

Correct Answer

A White play at 1 would make a large framework of territory at the top. Therefore, Black has to prevent this by playing there first.

Problem 32

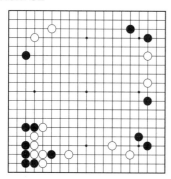 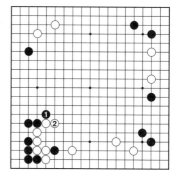

Correct Answer

Black 1 follows the principle of expanding a framework while reducing the size of an opponent's. It also prevents White from taking this point, which would produce the opposite result.

Problem 33

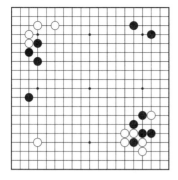
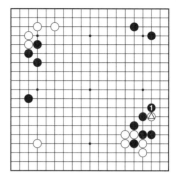

Correct Answer

"Secure weak stones so that they don't come under attack." This is the principle that should be used in solving this problem. Black 1 quells the marked stone so that it cannot run away and weaken Black's four stones. It also makes a strong position that works well with the corner enclosure at the top right.

Problem 34

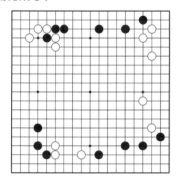
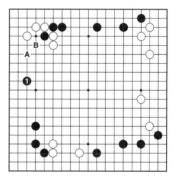

Correct Answer

It may seem as if Black 1 violates the principle of not approaching thickness, but, because of the lone Black stone above it, White is not as thick as it might appear. If White invades Black's position in the lower-left side, Black can make an ideal extension to A. White would have to respond because of the threat to link up with B, which would split White's stones, leaving the two in the center floating without a base.

Problem 35

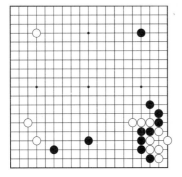 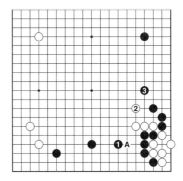

Correct Answer

Black should reinforce the bottom stones with 1. If White's three stones ran away by jumping to 2, Black stakes out territory on the-right side with the knight's move of 3.

If Black plays 1 at 2, White will attack the five black stones in the lower-right by playing at A.

Problem 36

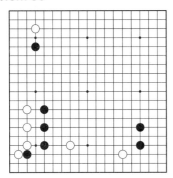 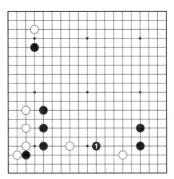

Correct Answer

Black has strong positions on the left and on the right, while White's two stones at the bottom are widely spaced. Such a position calls for an invasion, and Black 1 is the perfect point.

The reader might have noted that the upper-right corner is still empty, so there is a temptation to occupy it. However, White would reinforce by playing on 1, and Black would have lost the chance to seize the initiative.

Problem 37

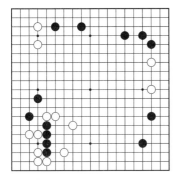 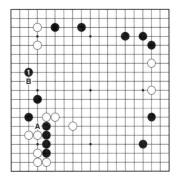

Correct Answer

Black must secure the stones on the left side with 1. This move not only stakes out territory, but also threatens the two white stones in the upper-left corner.

Black must not try to save the four stones in the lower-left by linking up with A. In response, White would extend to B, a big move because suddenly Black has no base and is under attack. Meanwhile, White is taking territory and strengthening the two stones in the upper-left.

Problem 38

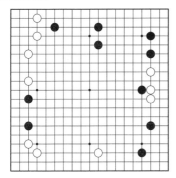 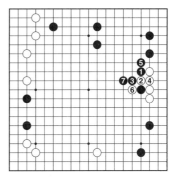

Correct Answer

Black should attach with 1. The sequence to Black 7 is inevitable and Black's framework expands and is reinforced.

Problem 39

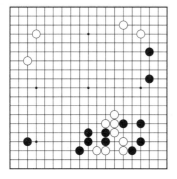 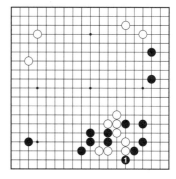

Correct Answer

Black 1 seizes the initiative because it robs the white stones of a base and reinforces Black's corner.

Problem 40

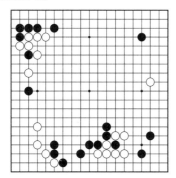 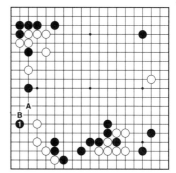

Correct Answer

Black's solitary stone in the middle of the left side is without a base, and White can attack it by playing at A, a move that would expand and reinforce the lower left corner territory. Sliding to Black 1 is a flexible move because it encroaches on White's area and also creates a base for Black on the left side.

Instead of 1, Black A might seem to be more solid, but White B would secure the corner and aim at the weak underbelly of Black's two stones. They would have a difficult time from that point on.

Suggested Reading

Unless noted, all suggested books are from Mr. Bozulich's Kiseido Publishing Company and are available through www.kiseido.com

In the Beginning by James Davies
This book covers all the basics, such as approach moves, corner enclosures, extensions along the sides, etc.

Opening Theory Made Easy by Otake Hideo
A Japanese master presents 20 principles of opening play.

501 Opening Problems by Richard Bozulich
Every aspect of the opening is covered and each problem introduces an opening principle.

Get Strong at the Opening by Richard Bozulich
The 175 problems in this book progressively cover many of the standard opening patterns, such as the Chinese opening, the *niren-sei*, the *sanren-sei*, and the Shusaku opening.

The Chinese Opening by Kato Masao
The Chinese opening is one of the most popular opening patterns played by modern professional players. This book is a systematic analysis by one of Japan's former top title-holders.

CHAPTER THREE

Tesuji—Clever Moves

Tesuji are non-obvious, skillful moves that separate, capture, link up and save stones and groups. They can suddenly tear apart shapes that seem to look good, or quickly revive those that might look bad.

There are about 50 different kinds, and knowledge of them along with the ability to see them instinctively during a game is a big factor in distinguishing strong players from weak ones. The only way to develop this instinct is through studying and solving as many problems as possible.

Shortage of Liberties

One of the most important concepts related to tesuji problems, as well to those of life, death and the endgame, is shortage of liberties. In these problems, the concept comes up again and again because it indicates the presence of bad shape, which is critical when the fighting gets to close quarters.

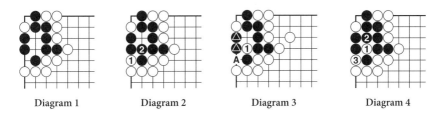

| Diagram 1 | Diagram 2 | Diagram 3 | Diagram 4 |

For example, White wants to kill the black group in Diagram 1. If there is a simple atari with 1 as in Diagram 2, Black will connect at 2 and have two eyes. However, in Diagram 3, White has a throw-in tesuji that creates a shortage of liberties for the marked stones. Black cannot connect at *A* because there is only one liberty left and White can capture on the next move. In Diagram 4, if Black captures with 2, White will atari with 3 and Black is left with only one eye.

Tesuji Problems

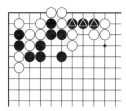

Problem 1
How can Black save the three marked stones?

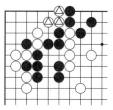

Problem 2
How can Black capture the three marked
white stones?

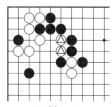

Problem 3
How can Black capture the two marked stones?

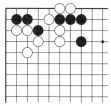

Problem 4
How can Black save the two stones
in the corner?

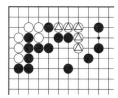

Problem 5
How can Black kill the marked white stones?

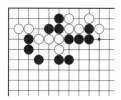

Problem 6
How can Black save three stones at the top?

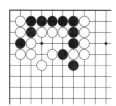

Problem 7
How can Black save the eight stones at the top?

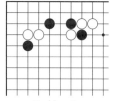

Problem 8
How can Black strengthen the isolated stones?

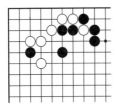

Problem 9
How should Black play in this position?

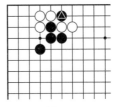

Problem 10
How can Black utilize the marked stone?

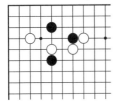

Problem 11
How can Black make shape for the scattered stones?

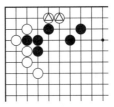

Problem 12
How can Black capture the marked stones?

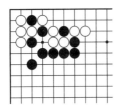

Problem 13
How can Black break into the top?

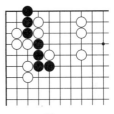

Problem 14
How can the Black stones be linked up?

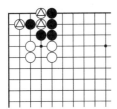

Problem 15
How can Black capture all the marked stones?

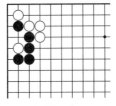

Problem 16
What is the most profitable move for Black?

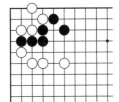

Problem 17
How can Black take the corner away from White?

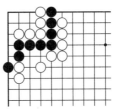

Problem 18
To save the black stones,
how can White be killed?

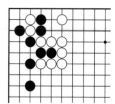

Problem 19

How can the black corner be preserved?

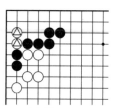

Problem 20

How can Black capture the two marked stones?

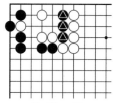

Problem 21

How can Black capture the marked stones?

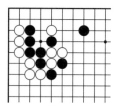

Problem 22

How can all the black stones be saved?

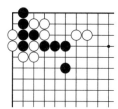

Problem 23

How can Black rescue the three marked stones?

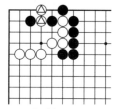

Problem 24

How can Black capture the marked stones?

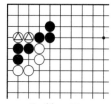

Problem 25

How can Black save the five stones in the corner?

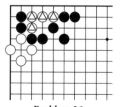

Problem 26

How can Black capture the marked stones?

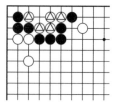

Problem 27

How can Black capture the marked stones?

Answers to the Tesuji Problems

Problem 1

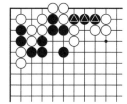 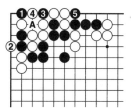

Correct Answer

The only move that saves Black's three stones is the "clamp" at 1. White must atari with 2. But now Black throws in a stone with 3, White captures with 4 and Black ataries with 5. White can't connect at 3 because of a shortage of liberties, so Black can capture at *A*.

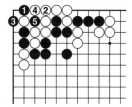

If White answers Black 1 with 2, Black ataries with 3. After Black 5, it becomes a ko, but White is at a great disadvantage in fighting it.

Problem 2

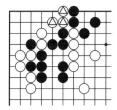 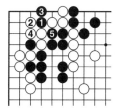

Correct Answer

Nudging in between the two white stones with Black 1 is the tesuji. After the exchange of White 2 for Black 3, White must connect with 4, but then Black ataries with 5 and three white stones are captured.

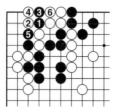

If White answers Black 3 with 4, Black ataries with 5 and White captures with 6.

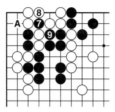

Next, Black throws in a stone with 7. After White 8, Black ataries with 9. If White connects at 7. Black *A* leaves White helpless.

Problem 3

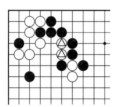
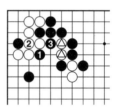

Correct Answer

Black 1 is the tesuji. If White connects with 2, Black 3 will capture the two marked stones.

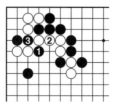

If White connects with 2, Black ataries with 3 and captures four white stones.

Problem 4

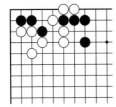   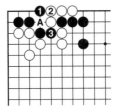

Correct Answer

The diagonal move of Black 1 threatens to cut at 2 so if White tries to defend by connecting at 2, Black cuts with 3. Because of a liberty shortage, White cannot atari at *A* and is dead.

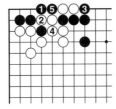

If White answers Black 1 with 2, Black ataries with 3. The white stones are short of liberties and can't connect at 5 so White must first connect at 4, but then Black captures two stones with 5.

Problem 5

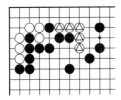   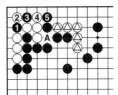

Correct Answer

Black should cut with 1. If White ataries with 2, Black ataries with 3. White must defend with 4, but Black blocks with 5. White can't cut at *A* because of a liberty shortage so the five marked stones are trapped.

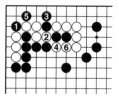

It may seem that White could live by cutting with 2 but Black will descend to 3. If White captures two stones with 4 and 6, ...

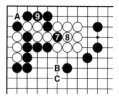

... Black will throw in a stone at 7 and then squeeze with 9. White connects with 10 (at 7) and Black connects at A. All the eyeless White stones will die and there is no escape by attaching at B because Black will block with C.

Problem 6

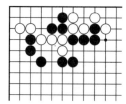
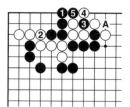

Correct Answer

Descending to 1 increases the number of Black liberties and threatens to cut at 2, so White must defend there. However, Black throws in a stone with 3, then ataries with 5 and if White connects with 6 (at 3), Black A captures six white stones.

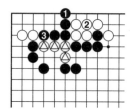

If White defends with 2, Black cuts with 3 and captures the four marked stones.

Problem 7

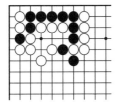   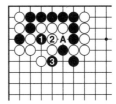

Correct Answer

Cutting with 1 is Black's tesuji. If White captures the cutting stone with 2, Black plays 3, and connects to the outside. White can't play at *A* because of a liberty shortage.

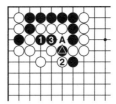

If White blocks on the outside with 2, Black plays 3 and captures three stones. White can capture the marked stone by playing 4 at *A*, but Black would capture four stones with 5 (at the marked stone). In any event, Black gets two eyes.

Problem 8

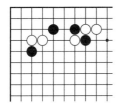   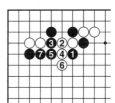

Correct Answer

The atari of Black 1 followed by the push-through of 3 and 5 is a tesuji combination that is often used to make shape for scattered stones. After the sequence to Black 7, White's two stones in the corner have been seriously weakened. Even if they manage to survive, Black will get a strong position on the outside.

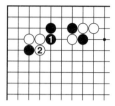

A Black attempt to push up with 1 is inferior to the correct answer. White "turns" with 2 ...

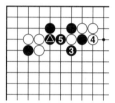

... and if Black now ataries with 3, White will ignore it.

Later, White might atari with 4. If Black captures with 5, it is clear that the marked stone adds nothing to Black's territory or shape. It only provokes White into making a good move.

Problem 9

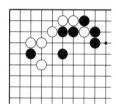
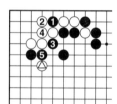

Correct Answer

Cutting with 1 is Black's tesuji. If White captures with 2, the moves to Black 5 are forced. Black ends up with a strong position on the outside and the marked white stone is neutralized.

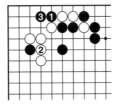

If White answers the cut with 2, Black's extension to 3 steals most of the corner.

Problem 10

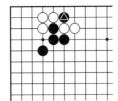

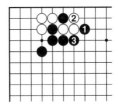

Correct Answer

Black's "nose" attachment at 1 forces White to capture a stone with 2. Next, Black blocks with 3. White's stones have been forced into a low position while Black is strong on the outside.

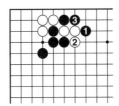

If White pushes out into the center with 2, Black links up at 3 and White's stones are split into two weak groups.

Problem 11

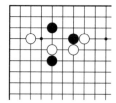   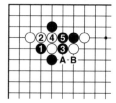

Correct Answer

Black should play a hane with 1. If White plays 2, Black ataries with 3, then blocks with 5, so Black's stones are out into the center. If White tries to block with *A*, Black can double-atari with a stone at *B*.

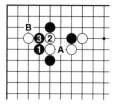

If White answers Black 1 with 2, Black pushes in with 3, threatening to capture two white stones with *A*. If White defends, Black will secure the corner with *B*.

Problem 12

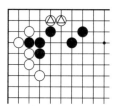   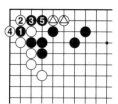

Correct Answer

Black's cut at 1 forces White to atari with 2 and then 3 and 5 trap the two marked stones.

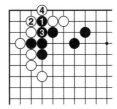

Black's block with 1 fails. White can link up with 2 and 4. If Black plays 3 at 4, White will cut with 3. Either way, all of White's stones are linked up.

Problem 13

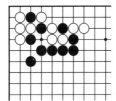
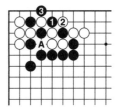

Correct Answer

With 1, Black ataries three stones as well as a stone on the second line. If White captures with 2, Black captures a stone with 3 and the white group on the left is dead. Because of a shortage of liberties, White can't atari at *A*.

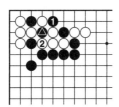

If White answers Black's atari at 1 by capturing the marked stone with 2, Black can throw in and capture four white stones.

Problem 14

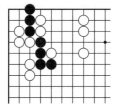 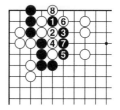

Correct Answer

Black should attach at 1. If White resists with 2 and 4, Black plays 5. White tries to save the stones by capturing one with 6 and 8, but ...

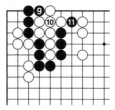

... Black ataries with 9 and 11 which leaves no escape.

Problem 15

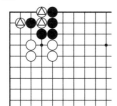 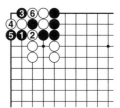

Correct Answer

Black should attach with 1. If White answers Black 3 by descending to 4, Black ataries with 5. If White tries capturing with 6 ...

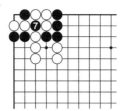

... Black 7 captures three white stones, and traps the two on the left.

Problem 16

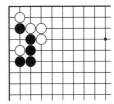 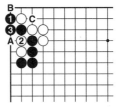

Correct Answer

The hane of Black 1 is the most efficient move. White 2 is futile because Black will connect with 3. There are no white plays at *A* or *B* because of the shortage of liberties and Black is still threatening an atari at *C*.

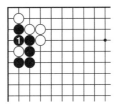

Black's connection at 1 is useless. Unlike the correct answer, it doesn't threaten White.

Problem 17

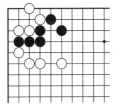 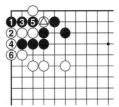

Correct Answer

Black's placement at 1 leaves White no choice but to connect with 2. Black 3 forces White to connect with 4 and 6, so Black can capture the marked stone and take the corner.

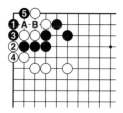

If White tries to link up with 2, Black can cut at 3 and White has to connect with 4. Next, Black attaches with 5 and White's stones at the top die. White *A* would be self-atari and Black would capture at *B*.

Problem 18

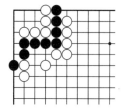   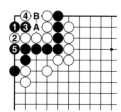

Correct Answer

The Black placement at 1 forces White to connect with 2. Black then exchanges 3 for 4, but, after Black plays 5, White is short of liberties. There is no play at *A* because Black will capture at *B*.

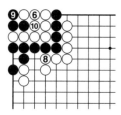

If White continues by connecting with 6, Black can ignore it and play 7 elsewhere on the board.

If White starts a capturing race with 8, Black plays 9 and White captures ...

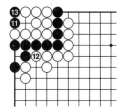
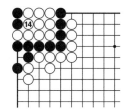
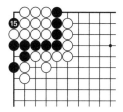

... but Black plays 11 and 13, and White loses the capturing race.

Problem 19

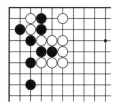
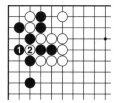

Correct Answer

Black should dip down with 1 and let White capture two stones with 2.

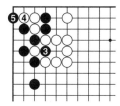

Continuation

With the recapture at 3, Black's territory on the left is secure. Next, White 4 is futile since Black answers at 5.

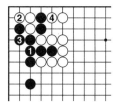

If Black tries saving two stones by connecting with 1, White turns with 2, forcing Black to connect with 3. The two black stones at the top can then be trapped with 4.

Problem 20

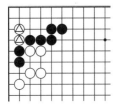

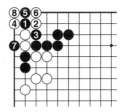

Correct Answer

Black's attachment at 1 is the tesuji. After the moves to 4, sacrificing two stones by descending to 5 is the key move. After White captures with 8 ...

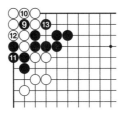

... Black throws in a stone with 9. The sequence is fatal for White.

Problem 21

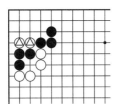

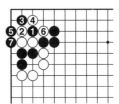

Correct Answer

Black should play the two-step hane of 1 and 3. If White captures with 4, Black squeezes with 5 and 7.

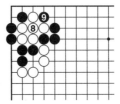

White 8 is futile since Black 9 leaves no escape.

Problem 22

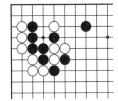 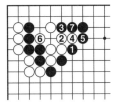

Correct Answer

Black ataries with 1, then squeezes with 3 to 7. White is helpless …

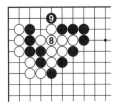

… since after the connection of 8, Black 9 traps the white stones.

Problem 23

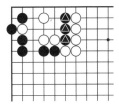 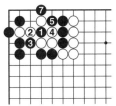

Correct Answer

Black's "wedge" in between the white stones with 1 is the tesuji. Even if White ataries from the left with 2, captures with 4, and fills in 6 at 1, Black can capture everything after playing 7.

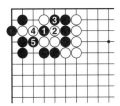

It is the same result if White ataries from the right side. Again, the fill-in at 1 is futile.

Problem 24

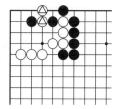 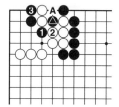

Correct Answer

Black should block with 1. If White ataries with 2, Black 3 captures two white stones. White can't capture at A because Black would recapture the marked stone.

Problem 25

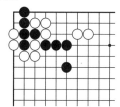 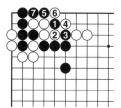

Correct Answer

After Black attaches with 1, the sequence to Black 7 is inevitable.

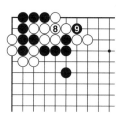

White connects with 8, but Black 9 captures the white stones.

Problem 26

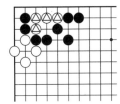 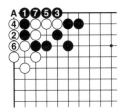

Correct Answer

Black's descent to the edge of the board increases the liberties of the group which is going to be crucial in the capturing race that will follow. White starts by eliminating the liberties of Black's group with 2 and 4, and Black does likewise with 3 and 5. But now White cannot play at *A* and must fill in with 6, which lets Black atari with 7

Problem 27

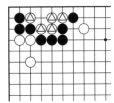 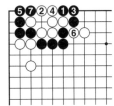

Correct Answer

Black starts with the hane of 1 and White tries to make an eye with 2. Black 3 and 5 make White 4 and 6 useless since Black ataries with 7 and captures the group.

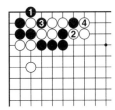

Black's atari at 1 is on the wrong side. White would cut with 2 and capture a black stone with 4. This way, White loses a stone, but saves the main body of the group.

Suggested Reading

Tesuji by James Davies

This book provides a myriad of simple examples.

Get Strong at Tesuji by Richard Bozulich

With 535 problems, the same kinds of *tesuji* are presented numerous times in different contexts.

501 Tesuji Problems by Richard Bozulich

Every kind of *tesuji* is examined in this book.

CHAPTER FOUR

Shikatsu—Life and Death

Positions that involve the life or death of groups constantly occur in games and the killing or saving of them often makes the difference between a win and a loss. In this vital part of the game, all go players agree that solving problems is the best way to develop a feeling for eye shapes and the ability to read many moves ahead.

A Short Review of the Basic Dead Shapes

Three-point eye spaces

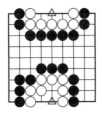

Diagram 1

In groups with three-point eye spaces, the marked spots are the vital points for both players. If White plays there first, the group is alive with two eyes. If Black plays first, it is dead.

Four-point eye spaces

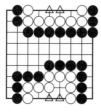

Diagram 2

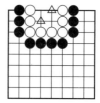

Diagram 3

Whether a four-point eye space group is alive or dead depends on its shape. White is alive in Diagram 2. If Black plays at one marked point, White can play on the other.

However, in the square four-point eye space group in Diagram 3, White needs two moves to live (for example, at the marked points), but Black needs only one inside move to kill it.

Five-point eye spaces

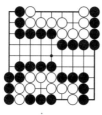

Diagram 4

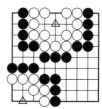

Diagram 5

In Diagram 4, the five-point group is alive regardless of where the "notch" is. That is, unless Black gets to play the three marked moves in an unusual ko. In that case, it would be what is called a seki ("se-key") since neither Black or White would want to play on the inside. For White, it would be self-atari, for Black it would leave White with a four-point living group. Under Japanese rules, neither side would gain points. As shown in Diagram 5, two other possible shapes are dead or alive when a Black or White stone is played at the marked spots.

Six-point eye spaces

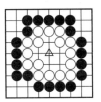

Diagram 6

Diagram7

Six-point eye space groups with the rectangular configuration in Diagram 6 that have no liberties are dead. After White 3, Black cannot play at *A* because of a shortage of liberties.

Diagram 7 shows the only six-point group that can die with or without outside liberties. This is called a "flowery-six" in Japan because of its shape. The marked spot is vital for its life or death.

Some Elementary Killing Techniques

Hane-Placement Combinations

One of the main techniques used for killing groups is to reduce the target eye space to a dead eye space. Two important tesuji combinations for doing this are hane and placement moves.

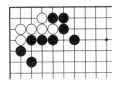

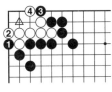

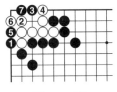

Diagram 8

Diagram 9

Diagram 10

In Diagram 8, Black can kill the white group in the corner with the two hane moves in Diagram 9. These moves reduce White's group to a five-point dead eye space so Black can play a placement tesuji on the marked spot.

White might try to answer Black's hane at 1 by turning at 2 in Diagram 10. In this case, Black would make a placement with 3. White must block with 4 to prevent Black from linking up on the right, but Black continues with 5. If White 6, Black 7 leaves the white group with only one eye. If White 6 at 7, then Black can play at 6.

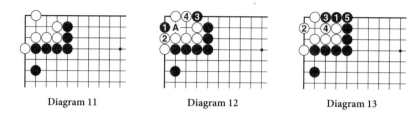

<table>
<tr><td>Diagram 11</td><td>Diagram 12</td><td>Diagram 13</td></tr>
</table>

There are times when a placement should precede a hane as in Diagram 11. Black should first make the placement of 1 in Diagram 12 because it threatens to cut at 2. After White defends with 2, Black can hane with 3. If White 4, Black can play at *A* to reduce the white group to a dead space. If White 4 is at *A*, Black will answer at 4.

If Black first hanes with 1 in Diagram 13, White can make eye shape in the corner with 2. If Black 3 next, White ataries with 4, and the group has two eyes.

The Throw-In Tesuji

Another important killing technique is the throw-in. This tesuji can also have the effect of reducing a group's eye space to a dead one.

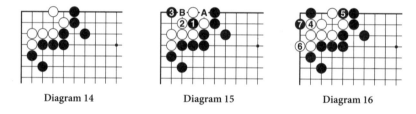

<table>
<tr><td>Diagram 14</td><td>Diagram 15</td><td>Diagram 16</td></tr>
</table>

Black can kill the white group in Diagram 14 by throwing in a stone at 1 in Diagram 15. Capturing it is the only way for White to resist, but if White tries to make an eye at *A*, Black ataries at *B*, or if White *B*, then Black can play *A*.

If White tries 4 in Diagram 16, Black ataries with 5. If White 6, Black plays 7 and White is dead. If White 6 is played at 7, Black can hane at 6.

Shortage of Liberties

Shortage of liberties is also an important consideration when trying to kill or save a group.

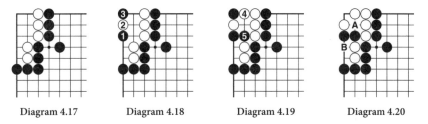

| Diagram 4.17 | Diagram 4.18 | Diagram 4.19 | Diagram 4.20 |

How does Black kill White in this well-known problem? After Black's sacrifice tesuji at 3, White's only chance seems to be to capture with 4, but after Black 5, there is no play at either *A* or *B* because of the shortage of liberties.

There are many other tesuji that are used to kill and save endangered groups, as will be illustrated in the problems that follow.

36 Life and Death Problems

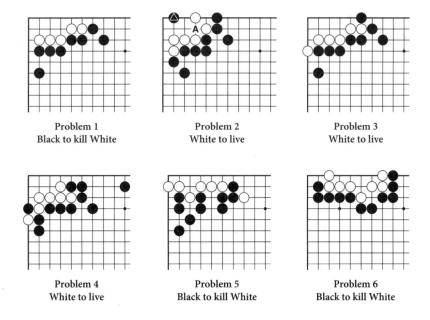

| Problem 1 | Problem 2 | Problem 3 |
| Black to kill White | White to live | White to live |

| Problem 4 | Problem 5 | Problem 6 |
| White to live | Black to kill White | Black to kill White |

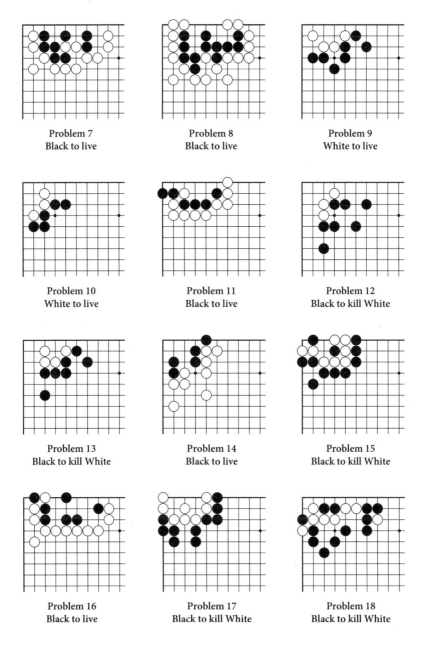

Problem 7
Black to live

Problem 8
Black to live

Problem 9
White to live

Problem 10
White to live

Problem 11
Black to live

Problem 12
Black to kill White

Problem 13
Black to kill White

Problem 14
Black to live

Problem 15
Black to kill White

Problem 16
Black to live

Problem 17
Black to kill White

Problem 18
Black to kill White

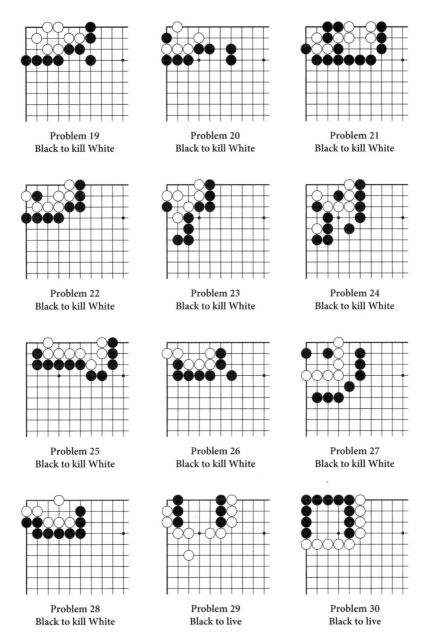

Problem 19
Black to kill White

Problem 20
Black to kill White

Problem 21
Black to kill White

Problem 22
Black to kill White

Problem 23
Black to kill White

Problem 24
Black to kill White

Problem 25
Black to kill White

Problem 26
Black to kill White

Problem 27
Black to kill White

Problem 28
Black to kill White

Problem 29
Black to live

Problem 30
Black to live

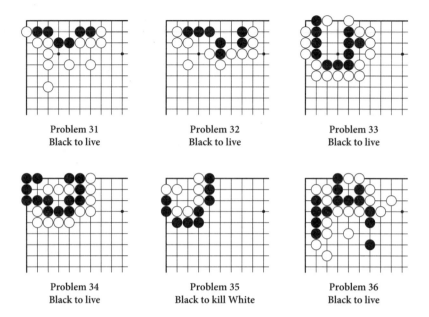

Problem 31
Black to live

Problem 32
Black to live

Problem 33
Black to live

Problem 34
Black to live

Problem 35
Black to kill White

Problem 36
Black to live

Answers to Life and Death Problems

Problem 1

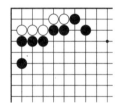
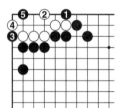

Correct Answer

Black plays a hane with 1, then another hane with 3. Black now makes a placement at the vital point with 5 and White cannot live.

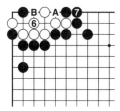

Continuation 1

If White tries to make an eye with 6, Black connects with 7. If White connects at A, Black ataries with B, forcing White to connect. This leaves a dead eye space.

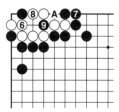

Continuation 2

If White plays this way, connecting at Black 7 is again the key move. If White 8, Black throws in a stone with 9. White can't connect at A because of a shortage of liberties. If White captures, Black ataries at A, leaving White with only one eye in the corner.

Problem 2

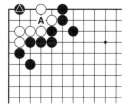
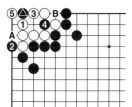

Correct Answer

In contrast to the throw-in example, Black's first move was the marked stone instead of the killing move at A. Now, White can live by "bumping" against the black stone with 1. Black hanes with 2, then throws in a stone at 4, but White captures with 5, and gets two eyes by playing at A or B.

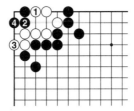

Failure

White 1 fails since Black can play on the key point of 2. If White 3, Black 4 and if White 3 at 4, then Black responds with 3. No matter what happens, White is left with a dead eye space.

Problem 3

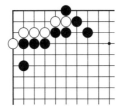

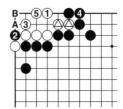

Correct Answer

White defends the two marked stones with 1. If Black throws in with 2, White doesn't capture but turns with 3. If Black 4, White 5. Black might try to create a false eye by playing at *A*, but White captures at *B*, making two eyes.

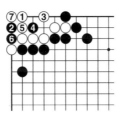

Failure

White 1 fails. Black will make placements with 2 and 4, then cut with 6. If White captures with 7 ...

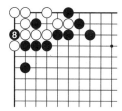

Continuation

... Black throws in a stone at 8, leaving White with only one eye.

Problem 4

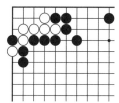 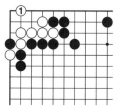

Correct Answer

White can live with 1.

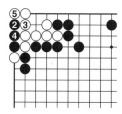

Continuation

If Black makes a placement with 2, White plays 3. Black connects with 4 and White captures three stones with 5.

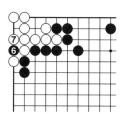

Continuation

Black might throw in a stone with 6, but White captures with 7 and the group has two eyes.

Problem 5

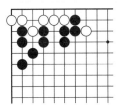 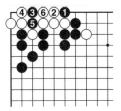

Correct Answer

Black first hanes with 1, then makes a placement with 3. White makes an eye in the corner, but Black 5 sacrifices two stones. After White captures with 6 ...

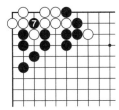

Continuation

... Black throws in a stone with 7, and White has only one eye.

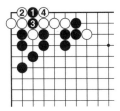

Failure

The order of moves is important. If Black first makes a placement with 1, then sacrifices two stones with 3, after 4 ...

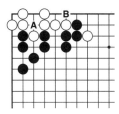

Continuation

... White can make a second eye either at *A* or *B*.

Problem 6

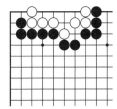   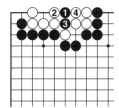

Correct Answer

The placement of Black 1 is the key point. White makes an eye with 2, and Black sacrifices two stones with 3. After White captures with 4 ...

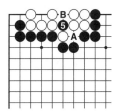

Continuation

... Black throws in a stone at 5. White cannot play at *A* because of the liberty shortage, and, if White *B*, Black *A* makes the point at 5 a false eye. The white group is dead.

Problem 7

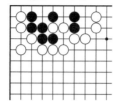 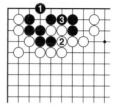

Correct Answer

Black should fall back with 1 to make an eye. White can only save two stones with 2, so Black can connect with 3 and the group is alive.

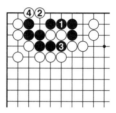

Failure 1

It is not enough for Black to capture two stones with 1 and 3. White makes a placement with 2 and links up in the corner with 4.

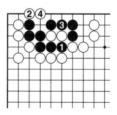

Failure 2

If Black first plays 1, White ataries with 2, Black captures with 3, and the situation reverts to the first failed position after White 4.

Problem 8

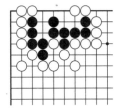 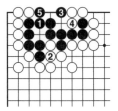

Correct Answer

Black 1 makes an eye. To stop Black from making a second eye, White has to connect with 2. Next, Black 3 is the key point. If White 4, Black has two eyes with 5 because White is short of liberties and can't atari the stone at 3.

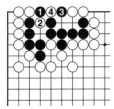

Failure 1

A ko results if Black plays 1 because White can play 2 and 4.

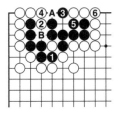

Failure 2

If Black captures with 1, White 2 is the key point. Black 3 threatens to start a ko by throwing in a stone at 4, but White connects there and can keep Black from making a second eye by continuing at either *A* or *B*.

Problem 9

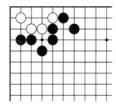
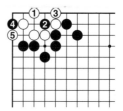

Correct Answer

White 1 is the key point. If Black ataries with 2, White descends to 3, and the black stone is trapped. If Black 4 comes next, White captures with 5 and has at least one more eye in the corner.

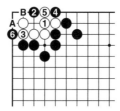

Failure

White loses if this 1 is tried. Black makes a placement with 2, then plays two hanes at 4 and 6. Next, White A—Black B, or White B—Black A kills White.

Problem 10

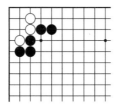
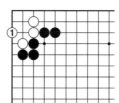

Correct Answer

White's group can live with the diagonal connection of 1.

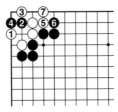

Continuation
If Black makes a placement at 2, White can live with the sequence to 7.

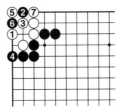

Variation
Black's placement at 2 fails. After White's throw-in at 5, it is useless for Black to capture with 6 since White will get two eyes after 7.

Problem 11

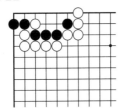

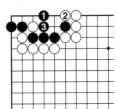

Correct Answer
Black should jump down to the first line with 1. If White 2, Black connects with 3 and the main body of stones has two eyes.

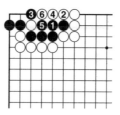

Failure 1

If Black connects with 1, the sequence to White 6 leaves Black with only one eye.

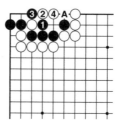

Failure 2

The atari of Black 1 also fails. White ataries with 2 and after Black captures with 3, White extends to 4. Black can't stop White from linking up at *A* because of a liberty shortage.

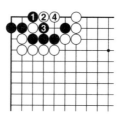

Failure 3

If Black ataries underneath with 1, White 2 and 4 revert to the same position as the second failure.

Problem 12

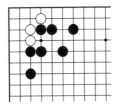 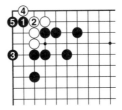

Correct Answer

"Peeping" with Black 1 is the tesuji. White has to connect with 2, so Black can play another tesuji by jumping down to 3 to link up with 1. If White 4, Black descends to 5, and the white group has no room to make two eyes.

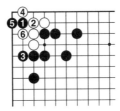

Failure 1

Instead of 3 in the correct answer, extending to this 3 results in failure. After White 4 and 6, Black's two stones in the corner can't link up to their allies below.

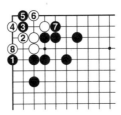

Failure 2

The order of moves in the correct answer is important. If Black first jumps down to 1, White will turn at 2. If Black now plays on the vital point of 3, the sequence from White 4 to 8 follows, and the result is two eyes.

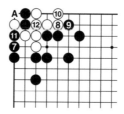

Failure 3

Instead of 7 in the second failure diagram, Black might play this 7. In that case, White can get a second eye at the top with 8 and 10. If Black ataries with 11, White will play 12, creating a shortage of liberties for Black. That is, Black can't capture with A because it is self-atari and White can recapture by playing there.

Problem 13

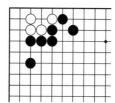

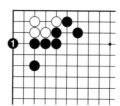

Correct Answer

In this position, jumping down to the first line with 1 is the key.

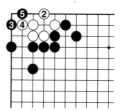

Continuation 1

If White makes an eye with 2, Black 3 and 5 prevent a second eye.

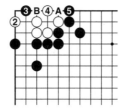

Continuation 2

If White answers with 2, Black makes a placement at 3. If White 4, Black descends to 5. If White plays *A*, Black ataries with *B* or if White plays *B*, Black ataries at *A*. Either way, White has only one eye.

Problem 14

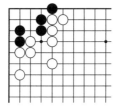   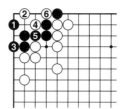

Correct Answer

As is often the case, playing on the 2-1 point is the key move. White 2 takes the other important point, but Black makes an eye with 3. Next, White threatens to link up to the outside with 4. It seems as if White has managed to set up a ko by throwing in a stone at 6, but ...

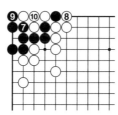

Continuation

... Black plays 7 and 9, forcing White to connect with 10.

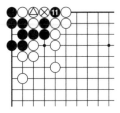

Continuation

Black now captures four stones with 11. If White captures that with the X-marked stone, Black plays on the other marked point and the group has three eyes.

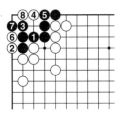

Failure 1

Connecting with Black 1 fails. After the sequence to White 8, Black is left with only one eye.

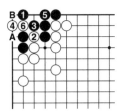

Failure 2

If Black starts by playing on the other 2-1 point with 1, White pushes in with 2, then makes a placement with 4. Black makes an eye with 5, but after 6, Black is short of liberties and can't atari at A or B.

Problem 15

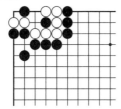 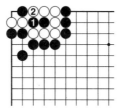

Correct Answer

Black first sacrifices two stones with 1. If White captures with 2 ...

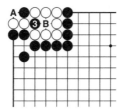

Continuation

... Black throws in a stone at 3, putting all of White's stones into atari without a viable reply. White cannot capture at A because Black will recapture three stones in the corner. If White captures at B, Black captures the eight stone group by playing back into 3.

Problem 16

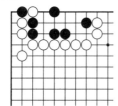 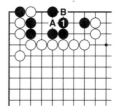

Correct Answer

Black 1 makes eyes at both A and B, so Black is alive.

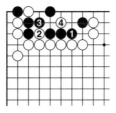

Failure 1
This Black 1 seems to expand the eye space, but White pushes in with 2, then plays 4 on the key point of Black's five-point eye space. This reduces the black group to only one eye.

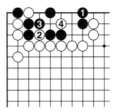

Failure 2
This Black 1 also results in a vulnerable five-point eye space which White 4 kills.

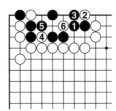

Failure 3
This Black combination also fails. After 2 and 4, White plays 6 on the key point of the resulting three-point dead space.

Problem 17

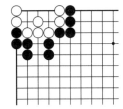   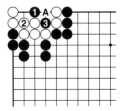

Correct Answer

Black 1 threatens to capture two stones either on the left or on the right. If White defends on the left with 2, Black throws in a stone at 3. If White captures at *A*, Black captures three stones by playing back in at 3.

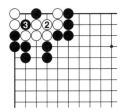

Variation

Similarly, if White connects on the right with 2, Black throws in at 3 and White loses three stones after the capture.

Problem 18

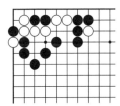   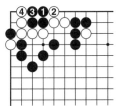

Correct Answer

Black 1 aims to leave the white group with a four- or five-point dead eye space. For example, if White ataries with 2, Black plays 3. After White captures with 4, Black is left with a four-point eye space because ...

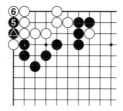

Continuation

... Black next plays 5. If White captures these two stones, Black throws in at the marked stone and White is dead.

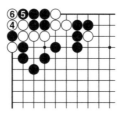

Variation

If this White 4, Black 5 makes a dead five-point eye space ...

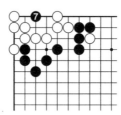

Continuation

... and Black 7 kills the group.

Problem 19

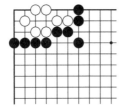
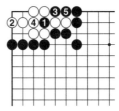

Correct Answer

Throwing in a stone at Black 1 is the tesuji and White can't make an eye by playing at 5 because of self-atari. If White tries to make an eye in the corner with 2, Black 3 and 5 destroy the potential one at 1.

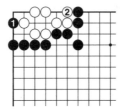

Failure

Black 1 stops White from making an eye in the corner, but White's group gets two eyes with 2.

Problem 20

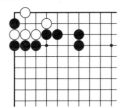
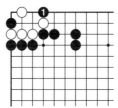

Correct Answer

Attaching underneath with Black 1 is the key move.

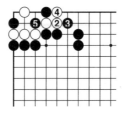

Continuation

If White tries to run away with 2, Black blocks with 3. After 4, Black ataries the two white groups with 5. One must die.

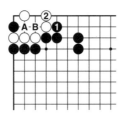

Failure

Black 1 fails. After a descent to the first line with 2, White's group in the corner is alive since, if Black *A*, White *B* or vice-versa.

Problem 21

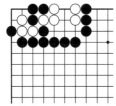
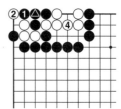

Correct Answer

Black's tesuji is at 1. If White captures with 2, Black plays 3 at the marked stone. After White makes an eye with 4 ...

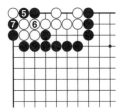

Continuation

... Black ataries the stone on the 1-1 point with 5. If White 6, Black captures the stone in the corner with 7.

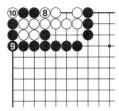

Continuation

White ataries with 8, Black connects with 9 and White captures with 10 ...

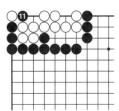

Continuation

... but Black recaptures with 11, leaving White with only one eye.

Problem 22

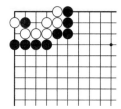 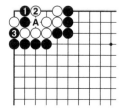

Correct Answer

Descending to Black 1 is the key move. White hopes to make an eye on the right by attacking the two black stones with 2, but after Black 3, there is no approaching at *A* because of the liberty shortage.

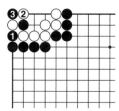

Failure

If Black ataries with 1, White ataries with 2. Black can capture with 3, but now White can fight a two-stage ko to live.

Problem 23

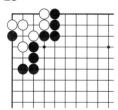 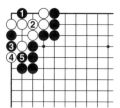

Correct Answer

Black 1 is the key point. White has to defend with 2. Black now creates a false eye on the left with 3 and 5 because ...

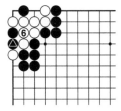

Continuation

... after White 6 takes two stones, there is only one eye left when Black throws in at the marked stone.

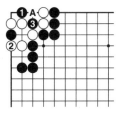

Failure

After Black 1, if White makes an eye on the left with 2, Black throws in a stone at 3. White can't capture at *A* because Black will take three stones by playing in at 3.

Problem 24

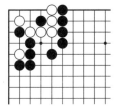

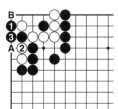

Correct Answer

Black should hane with 1. After 2, White can't capture the black stones in the corner because, when Black connects at 3, White cannot approach at *A* or *B*.

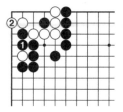

Failure

This Black 1 is a wasted move. White's group lives by descending to the key point of 2.

Problem 25

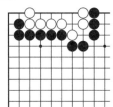 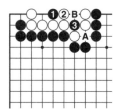

Correct Answer

If Black plays 1 there is no way that White can get two eyes. If White 2, Black throws in a stone with 3. If White *A*, Black captures at *B*. If White captures with *B*, Black ataries with *A*, turning the point 3 into a false eye.

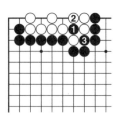

Failure

The order of moves is important. If Black first throws in a stone with 1, White will capture with 2. Black ataries with 3 and White takes the key point of 4. Now White has a chance to live by fighting a ko.

Problem 26

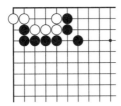 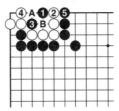

Correct Answer

Black makes a placement with 1, threatening to link up to the outside, so White blocks with 2. Next, Black cuts with 3. If White 4, Black 5 kills the whole group. White can't approach at A or B because of a liberty shortage.

Problem 27

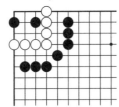 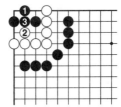

Correct Answer

Black 1 is the key move. If White 2, Black connects with 3, and gets an eye in the corner. The white stones will now die.

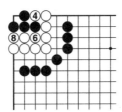

Continuation

If White persists with 4, 6 and 8, Black can ignore them and play elsewhere.

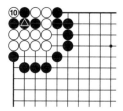

Continuation

Even if White 10 captures the four black stones in the corner, the result is a dead four-point eye space when Black plays in at the marked stone.

Problem 28

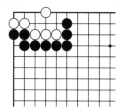   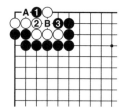

Correct Answer

Black should attach at 1. If White 2, Black turns at 3. Next, if White A, Black B or if White B, then Black A. Either way, the white group dies.

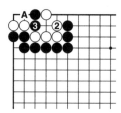

Variation

If White answers Black with 2, Black cuts with 3. White can't atari at A because the liberties are short.

Problem 29

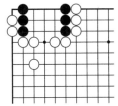   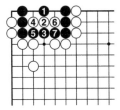

Correct Answer

Black can only live by playing 1 to get a seki with the sequence to 7. As mentioned before, in a seki, neither player wants to move and, under Japanese rules, neither player gains points. For example, ...

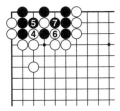

Failure 1

... if White goes all out to kill the black stones with 4, Black gets two eyes with this sequence to 7.

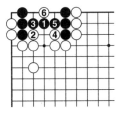

Failure 2

Black 1 fails because White forces with 2 and 4 to create a three-point eye space. White now makes a placement at 6 and the black group dies.

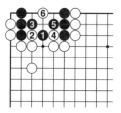

Failure 3

Black 1 on the third line also fails. For the kill, after 2 and 4, White again plays on the key point with 6.

Problem 30

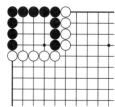
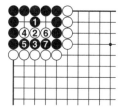

Correct Answer

The combination of Black 1 and 3 is the only way that the black stones can live. After the sequence to 7, Black's group is alive in a seki.

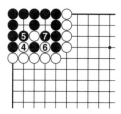

Failure 1

White must not play forcefully by taking a stone with 4 and 6. Instead of the seki where Black got zero points, Black's group now lives with two eyes. As well as gaining two points, White is in atari.

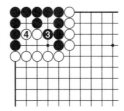

Failure 2

Making an eye with Black 3 leads to the death of the black group. White 4 takes away the only prospect of another eye.

Problem 31

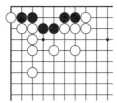
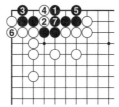

Correct Answer

The diagonal connection of Black 1 is the only move. If White cuts with 2, Black descends to 3. White plays 4 to prevent Black from making two eyes, but Black 5 makes one on the right. Next, White connects at 6, threatening the three stones in the corner, but Black 7 leads to the capture of 2 and 4.

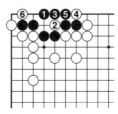

Failure

The diagonal connection of Black 1 fails. After White 2, Black can't play at 4 and has to atari with 3. White then ataries with 4 and after 6, Black is left with only one eye.

Problem 32

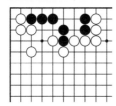   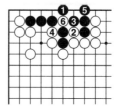

Correct Answer

Black can live by playing the diagonal connection of 1 and making an eye on the right with the sequence of 3 to 5. After White captures two stones with 6 ...

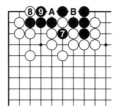

Continuation

... Black captures a stone with 7. Exchanging White 8 for Black 9 doesn't help because Black still has eyes at *A* and *B*.

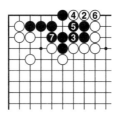

Variation

If White hanes at 2, Black will connect with 3. After the sequence to 7, Black is alive.

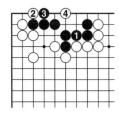

Failure

Connecting with Black 1 is no good. White hanes with 2, then makes a placement at 4, and Black's group is dead.

Problem 33

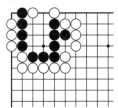
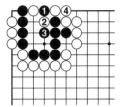

Correct Answer

Throwing in a stone with Black 1 followed by Black 3 is the way to make two eyes. White must connect at 4 ...

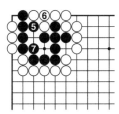

Continuation

... and Black ataries with 5 so White connects with 6 and Black makes the eyes with 7.

Problem 34

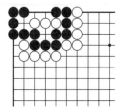 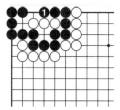

Correct Answer

Black should simply extend to 1. The result is a seki, so Black's group is alive with no points.

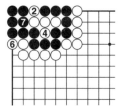

Failure

If White continues with 2, Black can ignore it and play elsewhere. White 4 can also be ignored, but when the last outside liberty is filled up by White and the group is atari, Black will have to capture with 7.

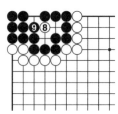

Continuation

This results in a living eye space. For example, if White 8, Black gets two eyes and five points with 9.

Problem 35

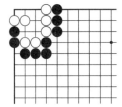   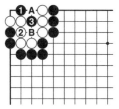

Correct Answer

Black 1 is the key point. If White 2, then Black 3 and White can't atari at *A* because of a shortage of liberties. If White connects at *B*, Black will connect at *A*. If White 2 at 3, Black plays 3 at 2. White is left with either a dead three-space or only one eye.

Problem 36

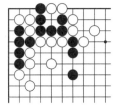   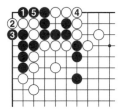

Correct Answer

Attaching with Black 1 is the key point for making a living eye space. If White descends to 2, Black plays 3 and White must connect at 4 before approaching the black stones. This gives Black time to atari with 5.

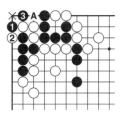

Failure 1

Black 1 is a mistake. White throws in a stone at 2. If Black 3, White captures at the *X*-marked spot. Black cannot play at *A* because it would be self-atari and therefore must win the ko in order to save the group.

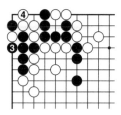

Failure 2

If Black captures with 3, White will descend to 4 ...

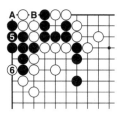

Continuation

... and if Black connects at 5, White will hane at 6. Black is short of liberties and can't approach at *A* or *B*. Black is dead.

Suggested Reading

Life and Death by James Davies

This book presents a logical, step-by-step development of life and death. All the standard shapes and tesuji are systematically analyzed.

Graded Go Problems by Kano Yoshinori 9-dan

Volumes 2 to 4 contain hundreds of easy to moderately difficult life and death problems.

Get Strong at Life and Death by Richard Bozulich

With 230 problems, this book covers every aspect of the topic. A special feature is a section with 78 life and death positions that arise in joseki.

1001 Life and Death Problems by Richard Bozulich

This book provides a vast number and variety of life and death problems for the intermediate player.

CHAPTER FIVE

Joseki—Local Skirmishes

The problems in Chapter Two were devoted to openings that involved the whole board. In contrast, joseki are local skirmishes that take place as the corners fill up. As revealed by tesuji and the potential life or death of groups, this is where the elements of good shape become vital, especially when the sequences spill onto the sides and out into the center.

For a series of moves to be considered joseki, they must produce a locally equal result for both players. However, joseki are also embedded within the fuseki so the situation on the whole board must be looked at with great care before choosing one.

As shown by historical game records, joseki and their variations have developed and been accepted or rejected over hundreds of years. This process goes on today with thousands being listed in standard dictionaries and supplements that are constantly being issued with the latest innovations. It would be a monumental task for anyone to memorize all of these, so better players rely more on shape and reading analyses than memory to come up with the best moves. It is in this spirit that the problems in this book are presented.

Many of the solutions are somewhat lengthy, so it is strongly advised to lay out the problems on a board before trying to work them out.

Joseki Problems

In each of these problems, find Black's joseki moves.

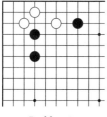
Problem 1

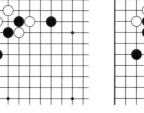
Problem 2

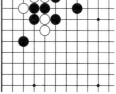
Problem 3

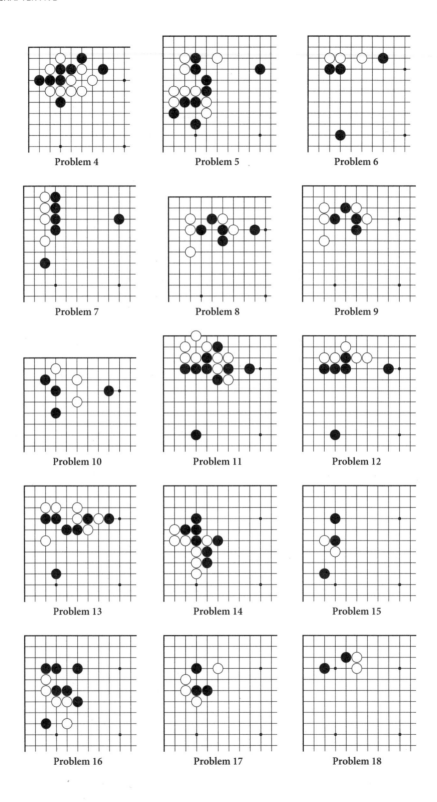

Problem 4   Problem 5   Problem 6

Problem 7   Problem 8   Problem 9

Problem 10   Problem 11   Problem 12

Problem 13   Problem 14   Problem 15

Problem 16   Problem 17   Problem 18

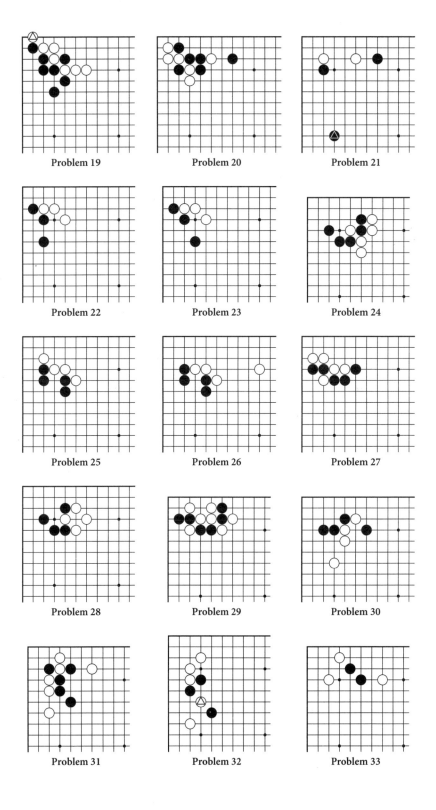

Problem 19

Problem 20

Problem 21

Problem 22

Problem 23

Problem 24

Problem 25

Problem 26

Problem 27

Problem 28

Problem 29

Problem 30

Problem 31

Problem 32

Problem 33

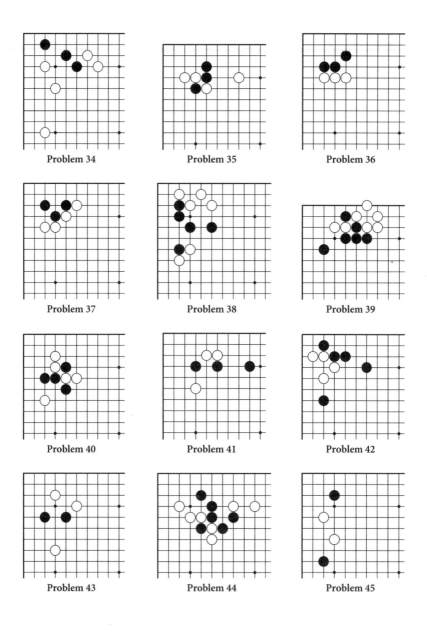

Problem 34

Problem 35

Problem 36

Problem 37

Problem 38

Problem 39

Problem 40

Problem 41

Problem 42

Problem 43

Problem 44

Problem 45

Answers to the Joseki Problems

Problem 1

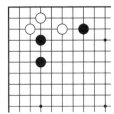
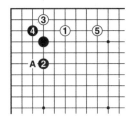

The Joseki

The sequence to White 5 is the beginning of the usual joseki. Black 2 can be at *A*, depending on the overall situation.

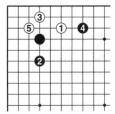

But after White 3, if thickness is wanted in the center, Black will play 4. In that case, it is usually advisable for White to then take the corner with 5.

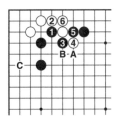
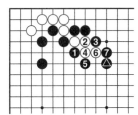

Correct Answer

White is solidly entrenched in the corner, so Black must go for influence in the center. The sequence to White 6 is the usual continuation. If the "ladder" is "favorable," Black will play at *A*—that is, if there is an edge of the board or a friendly stone such as the marked one that Black can herd White toward in order to make the capture. If it is not, Black will extend to *B*. Later on, White will look for a chance to slide to *C*.

Problem 2

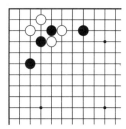 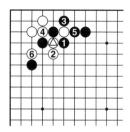

Correct Answer

Instead of 2 in the joseki of the previous problem, White played the marked stone in an attempt to foil Black's attempt to get influence in the center. Black should atari with 1, then capture a stone with 3 and 5. White 6 makes shape, but ...

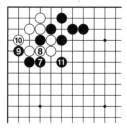

Continuation

... Black peeps with 7, then hanes with 9. If White blocks with 10, Black jumps to 11, setting up a squeeze.

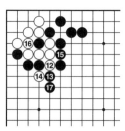

Continuation 1

Black still gets magnificent thickness in the center, but White gets at least 17 points of certain profit.

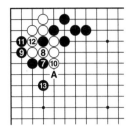

Continuation 2

If the amount of territory that White gains in Continuation 1 is not enough to compensate for Black's center influence, Black 9 can be answered by turning at 10. Black will exchange 11 for 12, then jump to 13.

Black ends up with strong positions on the left and at the top, but the white group that is poking into the center is still not alive. That is, if Black A, the white group will have only one eye. If threatened, White could retreat and get another eye in the corner but this would lose the initiative and gain little territory.

Problem 3

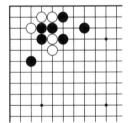 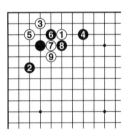 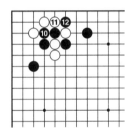

Deviating from Joseki

Black 10 was a mistake. This move should have been played at 12. Compare this with move 3 in the Problem 2 diagram.

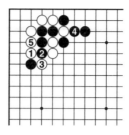

Correct Answer

White should set up a squeeze by attaching with 1 then atari with 3 and 5.

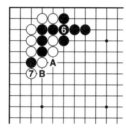

Continuation

Black connects with 6. White then secures the left side with 7. Later, if Black *A*, White *B* and White has taken full advantage of Black's misplay.

Problem 4

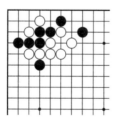
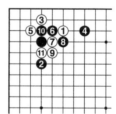

A Joseki Variation

In this variation, Black has played 2 on the fourth line. After Black 10 (which is not a mistake), instead of 11 in the continuation of Problem 3, White can push through with this 11 ...

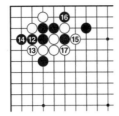

Continuation

... and continue with 13. Black gets territory, but White still has play in the corner ...

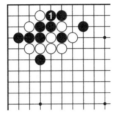

Correct Answer

... so Black should connect with 1.

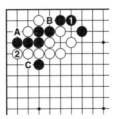

Failure

Instead, if Black extends to 1, White will block with 2, threatening to play at *A* or *B*. If Black 1 is at 2, White will simply turn at *C*, eliminating any effectiveness of the solitary black stone.

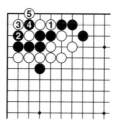

Continuation

After Black 2, White 3 is an effective move because ...

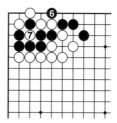

Continuation

... this leads to a ko when White captures a stone with 7. Given the dynamics of ko, White has the advantage by taking first and threatening to capture the black stones in the corner.

Problem 5

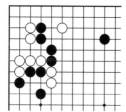 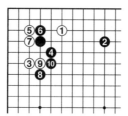 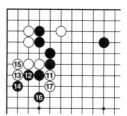

The Joseki

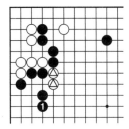

Correct Answer

Extending to Black 1 is the correct move and aims at attacking the two marked stones in the center.

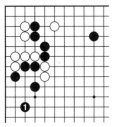

Failure

Black 1 is overly defensive.

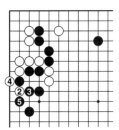

Continuation

The only merit of Black 1 in the failure diagram is that if White attaches with 2, Black ends up with good shape along the left side. However, this is an endgame consideration. The proper stage at which this joseki culminates is when the center becomes disputed, and that move is not center-oriented.

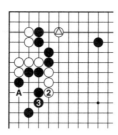

Continuation

Instead, White can strengthen the two outside stones with 2, forcing Black to extend to 3. White will now have an easier time making a living group in the center with the aid of the marked stone at the top. Moreover, White can still aim at the attachment at *A*.

Problem 6

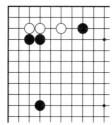

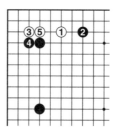

The Joseki

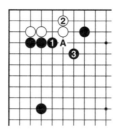

Correct Answer

In this basic joseki, Black 1 is the key point. White usually answers at 2 (or sometimes at *A*, which is a variation), and Black loosely links up with 3.

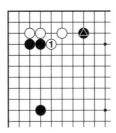

Failure

If White is allowed to take the key point with 1, Black's position suddenly collapses. The marked stone would be isolated from its allies on the left, and Black's two stones to the left of 1 have been seriously weakened.

Problem 7

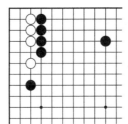

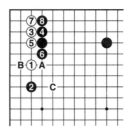

Failure

The sequence to Black 6 is the normal joseki (see Problem 6). White 7 is also a joseki, but Black 8 is a mistake. This move should have been at *A* and White would answer at *B*. Next, to emphasize the center, Black can play *C*, or, if the concern is about territory at the top, 8 can be played. Either way, all of Black's stones are working effectively.

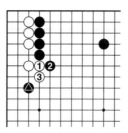

Correct Answer

Given the mistake, White should push up with 1 in order to isolate the marked stone from its allies. If Black 2, White turns at 3. Even though this move makes a clumsy empty triangle, it is the most effective way to play because ...

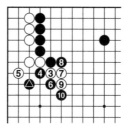

Failure 1

... the hane of White 3 is the move that would normally be played. However, the presence of the marked stone enables Black to cut with 4. White has to defend with 5, so Black can attack with 6 to 10 and White ends up with a heavy group floating in the center.

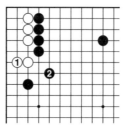

Failure 2

White 1 is submissive. The simple knight's move of 2 would loosely link up all of Black's stones.

Problem 8

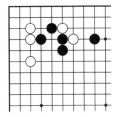 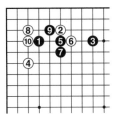

The Joseki

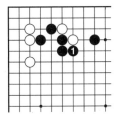

Correct Answer

Black should block White's ability to extend into the center. White should then play elsewhere.

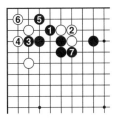

Failure

If White answers Black 9 in the joseki at 2, Black will threaten White's corner with 3 and 5, then turn at 7, trapping three white stones.

Problem 9

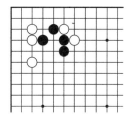 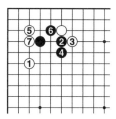

The Joseki

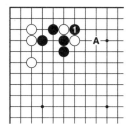

Correct Answer

When there is no stone in the vicinity of *A*, unlike in Problem 8, the correct move is to cut with 1. Black now has a solid and secure position.

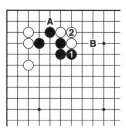

Failure

Playing at Black 1 is inappropriate in this position. White will connect at 2 and the three stones on the right are now secure. They can either link up with a hane at *A* or expand along the top by jumping to *B*.

Problem 10

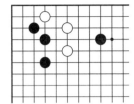
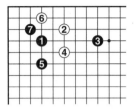

The Joseki

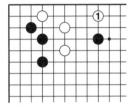

Correct Answer

White's joseki move is the long slide to 1.

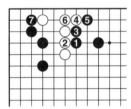

Failure

If White plays elsewhere, Black will attack with 1 to 5. After White connects at 6, Black blocks at 7. Now, the white stones don't have eyes and will have to make them in the center.

Problem 11

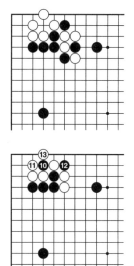

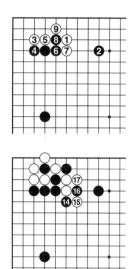

The Joseki

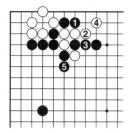

Correct Answer

Black should next atari with 1. White has to extend to 2 and Black connects with 3. White plays the diagonal move of 4, and Black finishes off the joseki by extending to 5.

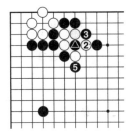

Variation

After Black 1, White might be tempted to capture the marked stone with 2, but Black's squeeze with 3 forces White to fill in with 4 at the marked stone. Next, Black 5 puts the group into atari, so this maneuver will be successful only if there is a stone that White can run to in the resulting ladder.

Problem 12

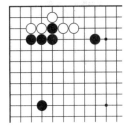 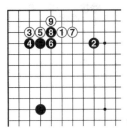

The Joseki

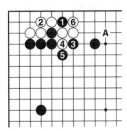

Correct Answer 1

Black should first cut with 1, forcing White to connect with 2. Black next attaches with 3. White pushes in with 4 to create defects in Black's position, but then retreats to 6. Later, White can aim at A to expand and gain territory at the top, but Black would get a thick position facing the center.

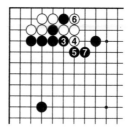

Black could also turn with 3. After exchanging 4 for 5, White must quell the black stone along the edge with 6. Again, Black exchanges a thick position in the center while White takes profit.

Problem 13

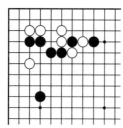

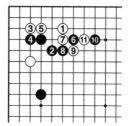

The Joseki

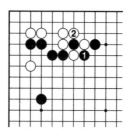

Correct Answer
Black 1 is a double atari, so White has to capture with 2.

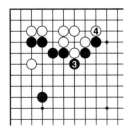

Continuation
Black now ataries with 3, White expands at the top with 4 and ...

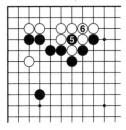

... Black will capture with 5. Fighting the ko at this early stage of the game is unreasonable, so White will connect at 6. Black ends up with a thick position in the center and White gets territory.

Problem 14

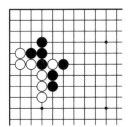 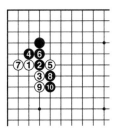 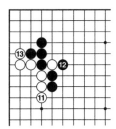

The Joseki

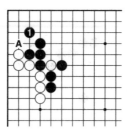

Correct Answer

Black should play the diagonal move of 1 to firmly secure the corner. Later, *A* can be aimed at by both sides, but this is an endgame move.

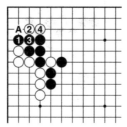

Failure

The first instinct for many players would be to block at Black 1, but White could wrest the corner from Black by peeping with 2 and extending to 4. White *A*, threatening to link up, is a "privilege", so the group will have no trouble living.

Problem 15

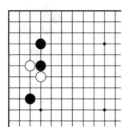
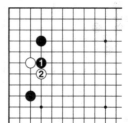

The Joseki

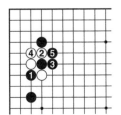
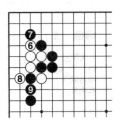
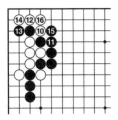

Correct Answer

Black should cut with 1 and keep White confined to the side while gaining considerable outside influence. This is a joseki, however, because of the amount of territory Black has to give up.

Problem 16

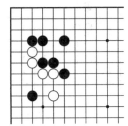
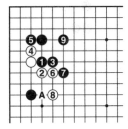

Deviating from Joseki

The moves to Black 7 are a joseki but jumping to 8 leaves White with a thin position. On the other hand, 9 leaves Black's stones thick and strong. White cannot afford to abandon this position and should play a move at A to strengthen the group.

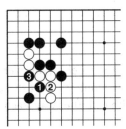

Correct Answer

White's mistake was to play elsewhere so Black can peep with 1 and then cut with 3. The two White stones above are captured and the four white ones in the center are floating without a base.

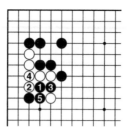

Variation

If White 2, Black ataries with 3, then connects at 5. The white group is dead.

Problem 17

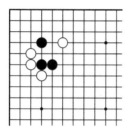

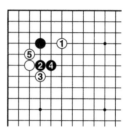

The Joseki

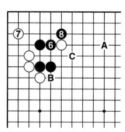

Correct Answer

This continuation completes the joseki. However, depending on the position, Black might play 8 at *A*. White would then push up at *B*, and Black would stake out the territory at the top with *C*. Either way, each side secures a stable position.

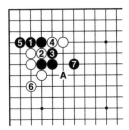
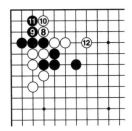

Failure

Black 1 is overreaching because White will cut through with 2 and 4. The exchange of 5 for 6 is natural, but Black must now jump to 7 because White A threatens to capture three stones.

After the moves to 12, Black is in trouble; the corner group needs a stone and the group in the center is floating without a base.

Problem 18

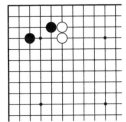
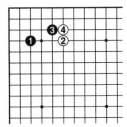

The Joseki

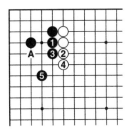

Correct Answer

Black should push up with 1 and 3 and then play 5 to develop a large and secure territory. To develop rapidly, Black often omits 3 and 5 but this risks the strong move of White A.

Problem 19

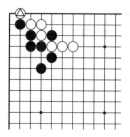 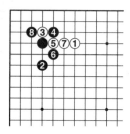 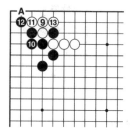

Deviating From Joseki

Instead of *A*, White should have played 13.

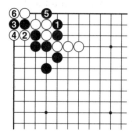

Correct Answer

To take advantage of White's mistake, Black should sacrifice the stone in the corner and block with 1. If White 2, Black will increase the sacrifice by adding another stone with 3. After the exchange of 5 for 6 ...

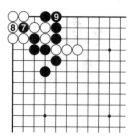

Continuation

... Black throws in a stone with 7, then connects at 9. White is dead.

Problem 20

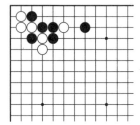

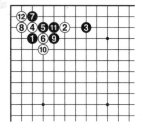

The Joseki

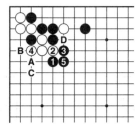

Correct Answer

Jumping ahead of the white stones with Black 1 is the tesuji. White pushes in with 2 in order to create cutting points, but then falls back to 4 for security. Black 5 completes the joseki. The correct answer to a future Black move at *A* is White *B* so to avoid this possibility, White might make the big move of a jump to *C*.

Instead of 5, Black *D* is also a joseki.

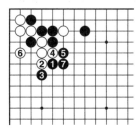

Failure 1

White must not push with 2 because Black will block with 3. After the sequence to 6, Black will connect at 7 and White's options for expanding along the left side are limited.

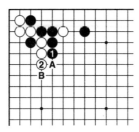

Failure 2

Pushing with Black 1 is a vulgar move since it induces White to expand along the left side. If Black persists with A, White is only too happy to comply with B. On the other hand, White A could be a big move, but it depends on the position below it.

Problem 21

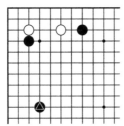

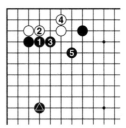

Correct Answer

In contrast to Black's move 5 in the joseki of Problem 20, with the marked stone in place the correct move here is for Black to extend to 1. The finished sequence reverts to the joseki of Problem 6. All of Black's stones are working efficiently and White has secured territory.

Problem 22

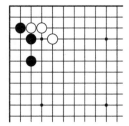 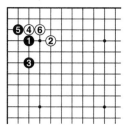

The Joseki

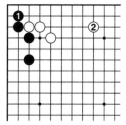

Correct Answer

Black has a solid position on the left, so there is no danger in extending into the corner with 1. After White extends to 2, Black can play elsewhere.

Problem 23

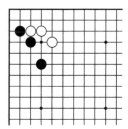 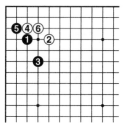

The Joseki

Black 3 of Problem 22 was a tight territory-oriented move while this Black 3 is center-oriented.

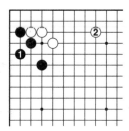

Correct Answer 1

By playing 1, Black can leave the position as it is and play elsewhere on the next move. Extending along the side is necessary for White's defense. If Black has a strong position in the upper-right, this extension could be narrower.

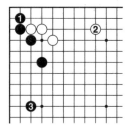

Correct Answer 2

Black 1 is also possible. However, after White extends to 2, Black must extend to 3 because the position above is a bit thin. White can then play elsewhere.

Problem 24

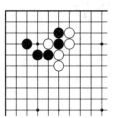

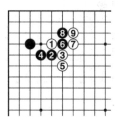

The Joseki

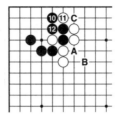

Correct Answer

Black 10 is the correct move and is the continuation of joseki. After 12, Black's corner is totally secure and Black will be aiming at the cut of A. This possible cut will be a source of annoyance for White who is left with a thin position, and will probably have to defend with B, even if there is a stone in place that makes the ladder favorable. Black also has the possibility of capturing a stone with C.

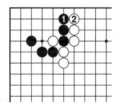

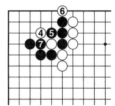

Failure

Descending with Black 1 is not a good idea. Instead of having the opportunity for capturing, White will block with 2, sealing off the right side and making the cut at A in the correct diagram less of a menace. White will severely follow up if Black 3 is played elsewhere ...

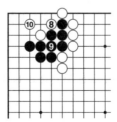

Continuation

... because White 10 will wrest away the corner.

Problem 25

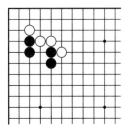   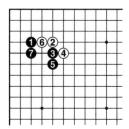

The Joseki

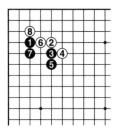

Correct Answer

Black should cut with 1. White has to atari with 2 and crawl with 4 and 6.

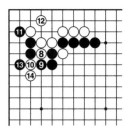

Continuation

After Black 7, the joseki continues as White cuts through with 8 and 10 ...

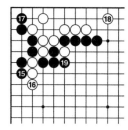

Continuation

... and Black lives on the left with the sequence to 17. Afterwards, White must anchor the stones at the top with 18 and Black has to secure the center stones with 19.

Problem 26

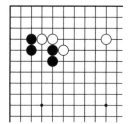

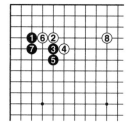

Deviating from Joseki

Instead of the hane of White 8 in Problem 25, White extended to 8 here. This was a bad move and Black will punish White for it.

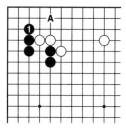

Correct Answer

Black should descend to 1 and threaten to slide to *A*, wiping out the territory White has staked out at the top.

Problem 27

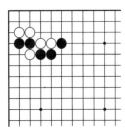 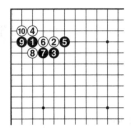

The Joseki

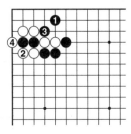

Correct Answer

Black 1 is the key point. Capturing two stones with 2 and 4, White continues the joseki sequence.

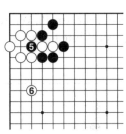

Continuation

Next, Black has to throw in a stone with 5 and White extends to 6, completing the joseki.

Problem 28

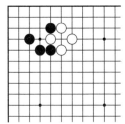 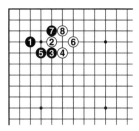

The Joseki

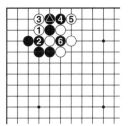

Correct Answer

Black should descend to 1 and secure a large territory in the corner. Black can exchange *A* for White *B* at anytime if there is a reason to fear a ko.

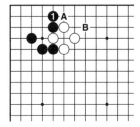

Continuation

After Black plays the marked stone, White might continue with 1 and 3. Black should respond with 2 and 4, and, after White 5, it becomes a ko. However, this is a bad ko for White because Black can resolve it by capturing a stone, leaving White with a big loss. Moreover, after this joseki is played, it is usually too early in the game to fight a ko and Black has the advantage by capturing first.

Problem 29

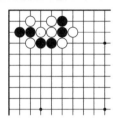
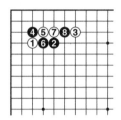
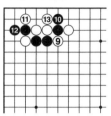

The Joseki

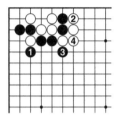

Correct Answer

Black should atari with 1, then, after White 2, atari again with 3. This completes the joseki and Black can now play elsewhere.

Problem 30

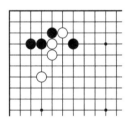
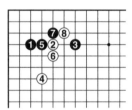

The Joseki

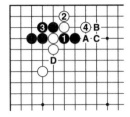

Correct Answer

Black should cut with 1. After Black presses with *A*, the attachment of White *B* is the key point. Black *C* and White *D* will follow.

Problem 31

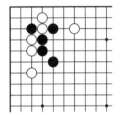 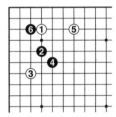 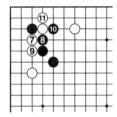

The Joseki

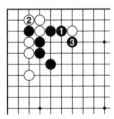

Correct Answer

Black should bump against the white stone with 1. White has to capture with 2, and Black 3 quells the white stone on the right, leaving good shape.

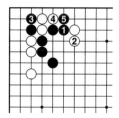

Variation

If White responds to Black 1 by "standing" with 2, Black 3 and 5 capture three stones. This is a good result for Black.

Problem 32

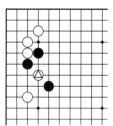
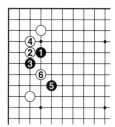

The Joseki

Considering that White has played two moves in this area before Black played 1, this is a good result.

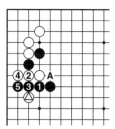

Correct Answer

Black should push through with 1 and 3 to sacrifice two stones. White has to descend to 4, and Black blocks with 5. Black now has a thick wall facing down the left side and has neutralized the marked stone. Later, turning at Black A is a strong move.

Problem 33

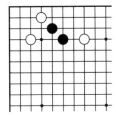
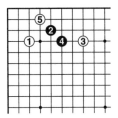

The Joseki

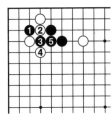
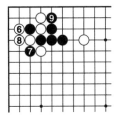

Correct Answer

Black should cut across the knight's move with 1 and the sequence to Black 9 can be expected.

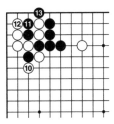

Continuation

If White captures a stone with 10, Black will capture two stones with 11 and 13.

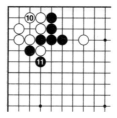

Variation 1

White could take the corner with 10, but Black 11 can capture a stone with a favorable ladder.

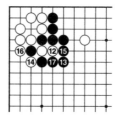

Variation 2

If the ladder is unfavorable for Black, White can be confined to the corner with a jump to 13. After 17, Black has a thick wall in the center.

Problem 34

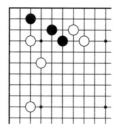 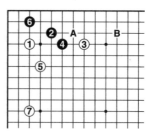

The Joseki

White would most likely have already played a stone around *B* before advancing to *A*.

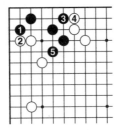

Correct Answer

Black 1 and 3 threaten White's territory on the left side and at the top. These two moves also stake out a sizeable territory in the corner, thereby guaranteeing two eyes. Black then finishes with 5, a tight move that ensures access into the center.

Problem 35

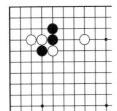

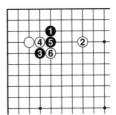

The Joseki

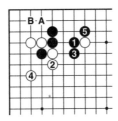

Correct Answer

Black should attach at 1. The sequence to Black 5 can be expected. Both Black and White have settled their stones. Later, White can aim to play A and Black can aim at B. Both are big endgame moves.

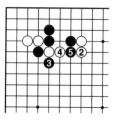

Correct Answer 2

Resisting with White 2 is also possible. Black will atari with 3 and start to thrust through with 5.

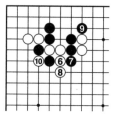

Continuation

With 7 through 9, Black neutralizes the two white stones while White 10 secures the left side.

Problem 36

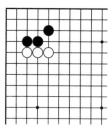

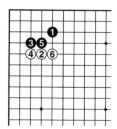

The Joseki

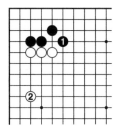

Correct Answer 1

Black 1 is a strong and steady move. White will respond by extending to 2.

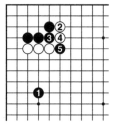

Correct Answer 2

Black could also play a pincer with 1. White will immediately attach at 2, to which Black must answer at 3 and cut with 5. This leads to a fighting joseki that Black must be prepared for.

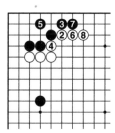

Failure

Responding to White 2 with Black 3 is submissive. Black is forced to play along the second line, while White builds impressive thickness in the center.

Problem 37

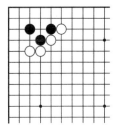
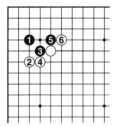

The Joseki

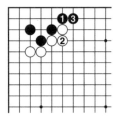

Correct Answer

Black should simply play a hane with 1 and, after White 2, extend to 3.

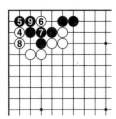

Continuation

White will continue by attaching with 4. The moves to Black 9 complete the joseki.

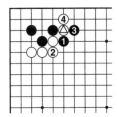

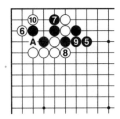

Failure 1

It may be tempting for Black to capture the marked stone by playing 1 and 3, but White increases the sacrifice to two stones then forces with 6 and 8 and takes the corner with 10. Later, White A can capture two stones and then play elsewhere by forcing Black, who cannot connect, to take the marked stone and White 4.

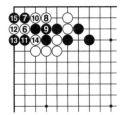

Failure 2

Black can't answer White 6 with 7. White would make a placement with 8 and cut with 10. The sequence to Black 15 is forced. Next ...

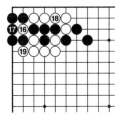

Continuation

White throws in a stone with 16, then ataries with 18. Black is finished whether or not 19 fills in at 16.

Problem 38

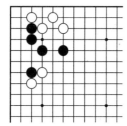
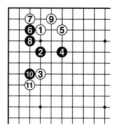

The Joseki

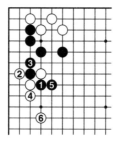

Correct Answer

Black should cut with 1. White builds a position along the left side with 2 to 6 while Black is secure. This is a joseki that would work very well for White if there was a friendly stone or group further down the left side.

Problem 39

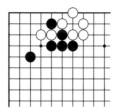
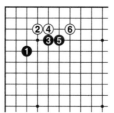
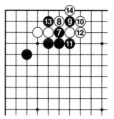

The Joseki

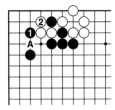

Correct Answer

Black 1 forces White to capture a black stone with 2. It also prevents White from expanding in the corner with a move at *A*.

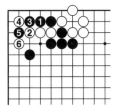

Failure

It is unreasonable for Black to try to take the corner with 1 and 3. White hanes with 4. Black tries to gain the upper hand by beginning a sacrifice two stones with 5 ...

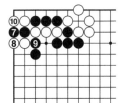
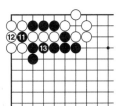
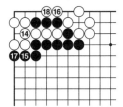

Continuation

… and 7 but it is useless. After Black throws in a stone with 11, White captures and Black squeezes with 13. White 14 connects and Black 15 starts the capturing race, but it is clear that White wins it after the atari at 18.

Problem 40

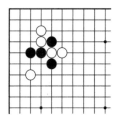 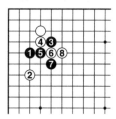

The Joseki

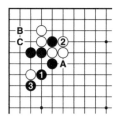

Correct Answer

Black defends against a cut and settles the left side with 1 and 3. Likewise, it is urgent that White take care of the lone black stone with 2. Depending on the positions in the adjacent corners, *A* could be the focal point of influence. Later, Black *B* or White *C* become big moves.

Problem 41

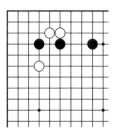 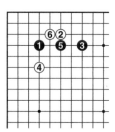

The Joseki

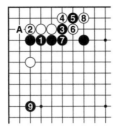

Correct Answer

Black 1 is the only move. It builds a solid wall and the extension to 9 neutralizes the lone white stone. Because of 3 and 5, Black *A* is now a big threat.

Problem 42

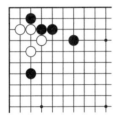

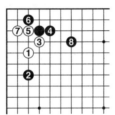

The Joseki

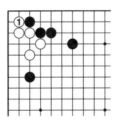

Correct Answer

White 1 is a solid and steady move that secures the white stones.

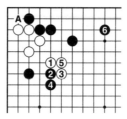

Failure

Moving out into the center with White 1 is another option, but after the sequence to 6, Black has been able to build strong positions on the left and at the top, while White's stones are still without a base. In fact, White would now have to go back and play at A because a black stone there would deprive the group of eye shape and leave it floating without a base.

Problem 43

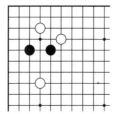

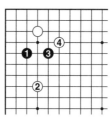

The Joseki

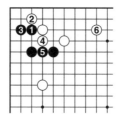

Correct Answer

Black has to stabilize with 1. The sequence to White 6 completes the joseki.

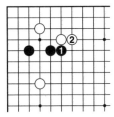

Failure

Trying to move out into the center with Black 1 is a bad move because it forces White to make territory at the top with 2.

Problem 44

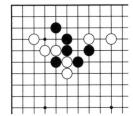

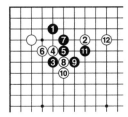

The Joseki

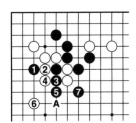

Correct Answer

The placement of Black 1 is the tesuji in this position. After White 6, trapping two stones with Black 7 is the safest move. However, Black might want to play at *A* to preempt a strong White move there.

Problem 45

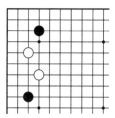
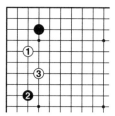

The Joseki

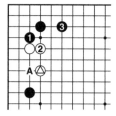

Correct Answer

Black should secure the corner by attaching with 1, and then extend tightly with 3. If the marked stone were at *A*, Black would still play the same way.

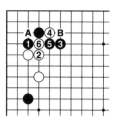

Failure 1

After the exchange of Black 1 for White 2, Black must not play the knight's move of 3. White would play 4, cut with 6, and threaten to play next at *A* or *B*.

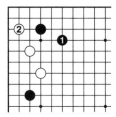

Failure 2
If Black plays the knight's move at 1, White can easily slide to 2 for security.

Suggested Reading

38 Basic Joseki by Kosugi Kiyoshi 8-dan and James Davies
This book analyzes the 38 most basic joseki, showing their main ideas and how to choose one in relation to other stones on the board.

Get Strong at Joseki Volumes 1, 2, and 3 by Richard Bozulich
Volumes 1, 2 and 3 present 544 problems in choosing the right joseki, their variations, and what to do afterwards.

21st Century New Openings by Kim Sung-rae 4-dan (Yutopian Press)
A survey of recent joseki innovations and their relationship to the fuseki in which they are played. It features hundreds of examples and 45 problems from professional games.

CHAPTER SIX

Chuban—The Middle Game

After the results of the opening strategies have become apparent, the middle game is where tesuji, life and death, attacks, invasions, defenses and preparations for the endgame become vital.

Important Elements of the Middle Game:

Fighting

One often-occurring feature of the middle game is fighting between eyeless groups. Sometimes these fights end in compromise, but often they end with one group dying. This is when tesujis can come to the rescue; they can help you kill your opponent's group or save your own group.

Weak and Strong Groups

Just as in the opening stages, players must be always aware of weak groups. If your opponent has a weak group you should look for a way to make profit while attacking it. But if you find yourself burdened with a weak group, it is usually more important to secure your own group before attacking your opponent's or making territory.

The Shape of Groups

Shape is usually the key for determining if a group is weak or strong. Good shape means that your stones are working efficiently, so it takes fewer stones to secure them. Morever, stones that have good shape can easily make the two eyes necessary for life.

Sabaki

As demonstrated on page 12, sometimes you will find your stones outnumbered on one part of the board and in danger of being captured. By sacrificing some of them using sabaki techniques, your objective should be to make good shape, rich in eye potential. They will then be able to make eyes or escape.

24 Middle Game Problems

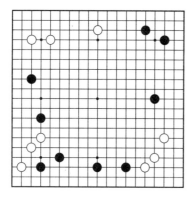

Problem 1 — Black to play

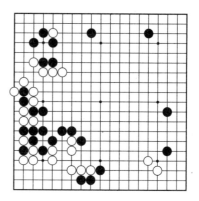

Problem 2 — White to play

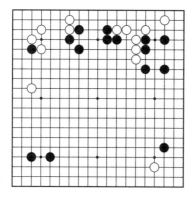

Problem 3 — White to play

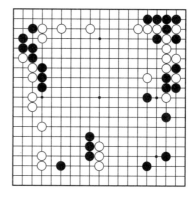

Problem 4 — Black to play

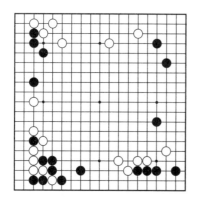

Problem 5 — Black to play

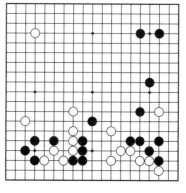

Problem 6 — White to play

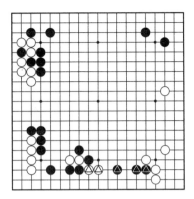

Problem 7 — White to play
The marked stones are in a life-and-death struggle.

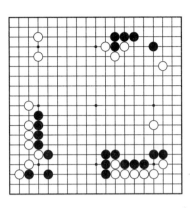

Problem 8 — Black to play
How can White get the advantage?

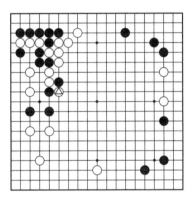

Problem 9 — Black to play
White has just cut with the marked stone.
How can Black make sabaki?

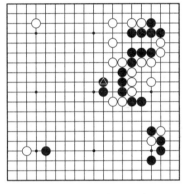

Problem 10 — White to play
After Black plays the marked stone,
how can White make sabaki?

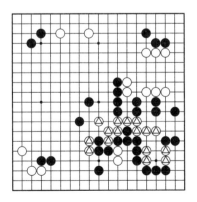

Problem 11 — White to play
White's marked stones don't have eyes.

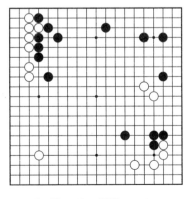

Problem 12 — White to play
How can White save them?

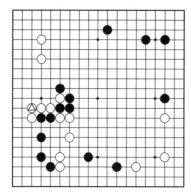

Problem 13— Black to play
How should Black respond when White

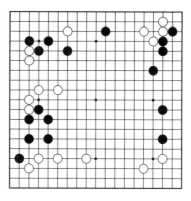

Problem 14 — Black to play
connects with the marked stone?

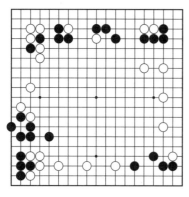

Problem 15 — White to play
Black's position is strong at the top.

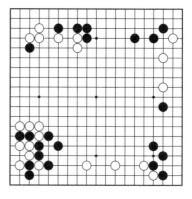

Problem 16 — Black to play
How can White make sabaki there?

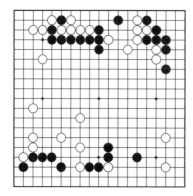

Problem 17 — Black to play
How should White invade the left side?

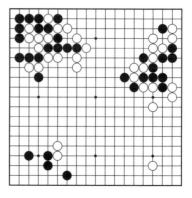

Problem 18 — Black to play
How can Black save the stones on the right?

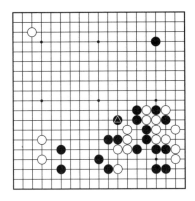

Problem 19 — White to play
After Black plays the marked stone, how can
White save the five stones at the bottom?

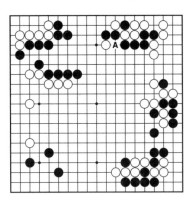

Problem 20 — Black to play
White is threatening to cut at A. Should Black
connect or is there a more profitable way?

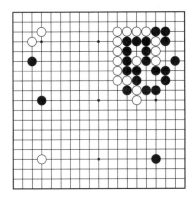

Problem 21 — White to play
How can Black save nine stones at the bottom?

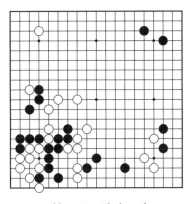

Problem 22 — Black to play

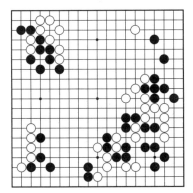

Problem 23 — White to play
How can White save the stones

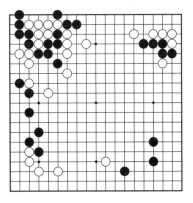

Problem 24 — Black to play
in the upper-left corner?

Answers to the Middle Game Problems

Problem 1

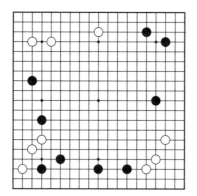 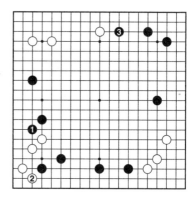

Correct Answer

The black stones on the left are thin, so Black should reinforce them with 1. Since this move also threatens the white stones below, White needs to defend with 2. Black can now take the big point of 3.

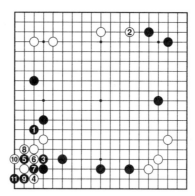

White's Failure

White cannot afford to ignore Black 1 and take the big point of 2. Black 3 is a severe move. If White now tries to make two eyes at 4, Black will force the sequence to White 10. After Black 11, White's stones in the lower-left don't have eye shape, so, while they struggle to live, Black will gain territory and influence.

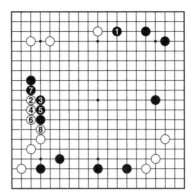

Black's Failure

If Black rushes to take the big point of 1, White will invade with 2. The sequence to White 8 can be expected. This is a huge loss for Black. White secures a large territory and Black is deprived of the territory that should have been taken by playing on the left side.

Problem 2

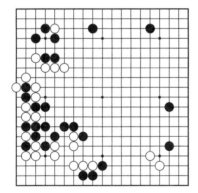
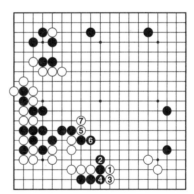

Correct Answer

White should attach with 1. Black will extend to 2, and White will peep with 3, forcing Black to defend with 4. White now cuts with 5, and then extends to 7. Black's groups on the left and at the bottom are without proper eye shape and will have a hard time making life.

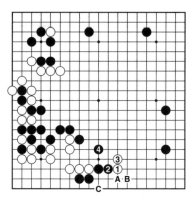

White's Failure

White 1 is a lukewarm attack. Black will bump against 1 with 2, then jump to 4. Black's stones here are much more resilient than in the correct answer diagram because they can live with the sequence Black *A*, White *B*, Black *C*.

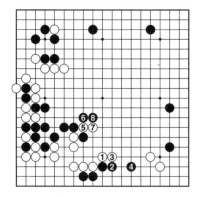

White's Failure 2

White's 1 and 3 are crude moves that help the black stones at the bottom live while weakening the two stones in the lower-right corner. If White now cuts with 5, Black can atari from above with 6 and press with 8.

Problem 3

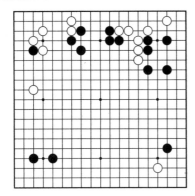 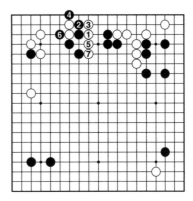

Correct Answer

White should attach with 1. If Black descends to 2, White will block with 3. The exchange to Black 6 can be expected, but, after White 7, the three black stones to the right have been isolated and are under attack. If Black 2 at 5, White will atari with 2, and Black will end up with an even larger vulnerable group.

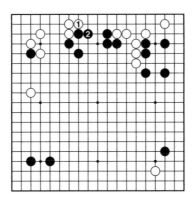

White's Failure

This White 1 is wrong because it induces Black to extend to 2, leaving an ideal shape. White has nothing to attack and has lost the initiative.

Problem 4

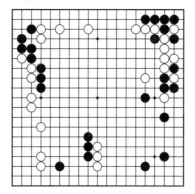 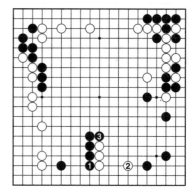

Correct Answer

The block of Black 1 is important because it secures a base and forces White to make a base as well by extending to 2. Now Black can turn with 3 to establish a strong presence in the center. This move is known as the "$1,000 turn" because of the powerful influence it projects into the center.

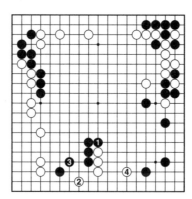

Black's Failure 1

Even though it is big, turning first at 1 is premature because the security of the group is more important. White will slide to 2, gouging out Black's base and forcing the defensive move of 3. White can then extend to 4 to form a base.

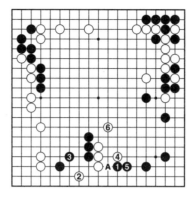

Black's Failure 2

Making a "checking extension" with this Black 1 is also the wrong strategy. Again White exchanges 2 for Black 3, then attaches with 4. Black must defend with 5, so White can move out into the center with 6. Black's stones are eyeless, and settling them will be a burden. White, on the other hand, can quickly get eye shape by playing at *A* if needed.

Problem 5

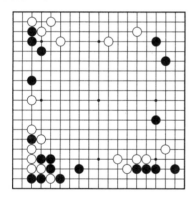 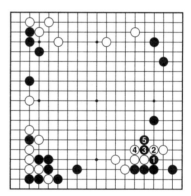

Correct Answer

Black should cut through with 1 and 3. If White ataries with 4, Black extends to 5 to secure territory on the lower-right side.

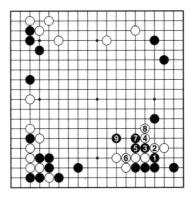

White's Failure

If White answers Black 3 with the atari of 4, Black 5 is atari, so White must connect with 6. After Black 7 and 9, White is split into two weak groups.

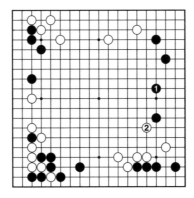

Black's Failure

Defending the right side with 1 is an overly passive move that fails to take the initiative. By jumping to 2, White's stones are connected and will have no trouble warding off a black attack.

Problem 6

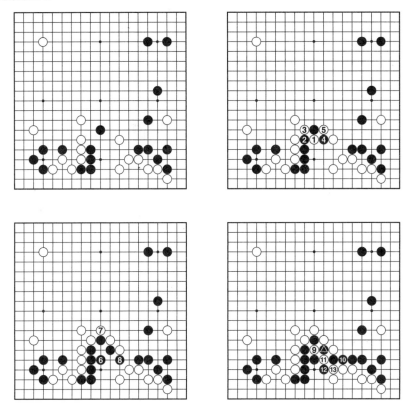

Correct Answer

Attaching across the knight's move with White 1 is the tesuji. If Black 2, White cuts with 3, and White 5 produces a double-atari.

Next, Black captures with 6 and White ataries with 7. Black's only resistance is with 8.

However, White can now capture with 9. Black can't allow White to play at 10 and must connect there. White then captures the marked stone with 11 and cuts with 13, so Black has to fight a ko by capturing at the marked stone with 14. Black has many adjacent ko threats and can probably live, but will end up losing the initiative. Meanwhile, White has built a strong position in the center

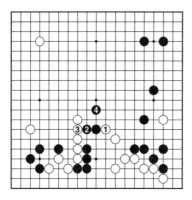
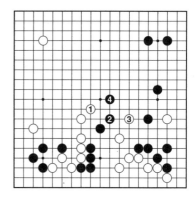

Two White Failures

These diagonal moves are lackluster because, in both cases, Black gets stones out into the center with 2 and 4 and White has failed to gain any advantage.

Problem 7

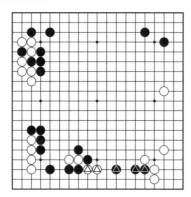
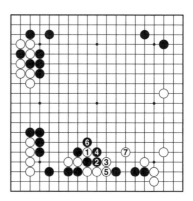

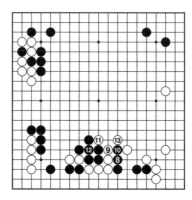

Correct Answer

White should atari with 1. Black has to escape with 2, and White ataries again with 3. After White 5, Black has to capture with 6, but White 7 traps the three black stones in the lower-right.

Black's efforts to escape with 8 and 10 are futile. White ataries with 11 and Black can't break through White's blockade.

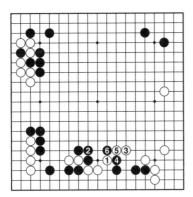 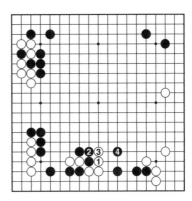

Two White Failures

These moves are both dull. On the left, Black simply secures the stones by connecting at 2. Attempting to trap the black stones with White 3 is unreasonable since Black cuts through with 4 and 6, trapping the three white stones.

The atari of the other White 1 also doesn't succeed. After White 3, Black jumps to 4 and White will be at a disadvantage in the upcoming fighting in the center.

Problem 8

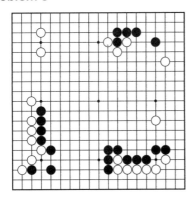 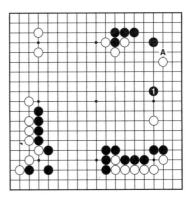

Correct Answer

Black's stones at the bottom and top are strong, while White's stones in between are thin. In positions such as this, Black should immediately invade with 1.

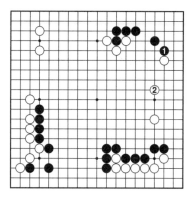

Black's Failure

This diagonal attachment might look good because it defends the corner, but White would then play 2 to establish a position on the right side. This neutralizes the influence of Black's strong position at the bottom.

Problem 9

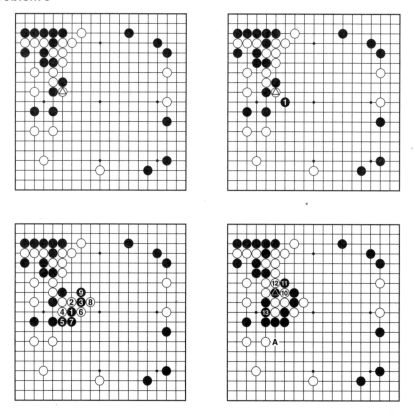

Correct Answer

Black can make sabaki by jumping ahead of the marked stone with 1.

White has to resist with 2 and 4 and the sequence to 14 is forced as White connects at the marked stone. Next, Black can extend to *A* and will have no trouble getting eyes in the center. Meanwhile White has ended up with a clump of stones while the black stones at 3, 9, and 11 can still create problems.

Problem 10

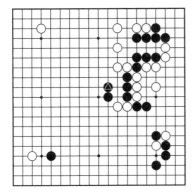
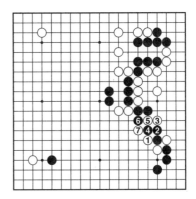

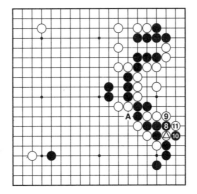

Correct Answer

White should atari with 1, then attach with 3. If Black pushes out with 4, Black must play the sequence to 12 (at the marked stone). White *A* traps the three black stones, saving the group.

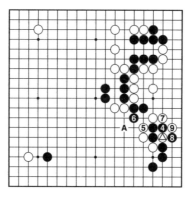

Variation

If Black retreats with 4, the sequence to Black 10 (at the marked stone) can be expected. White *A* traps the three black stones, saving the group and right-side territory.

Problem 11

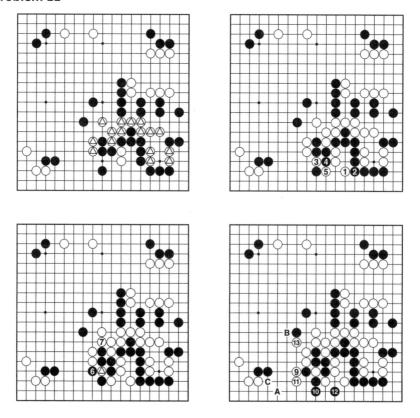

Correct Answer

White must first play 1, forcing Black to connect with 2. White now wedges in with the key move of 3.

Next, White squeezes with 5 and 7 forcing Black to connect with 8 (at the marked stone) and then sacrifices the four stones on the right with 9 and 11. After Black 12, White defends the cutting points with 13 and has made sabaki. That is, the group can be saved by linking up with *A*, or get out into the center in good shape with the hane of *B* in case Black plays *C*.

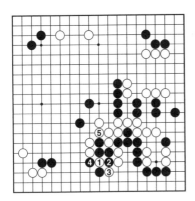
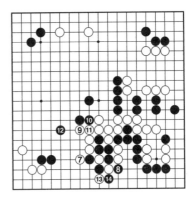

White's Failure

Omitting White 1 of the correct answer is a mistake because, after Black 8, White has to defend with 9. Next, Black forces with 10, then traps the white stones with 12.

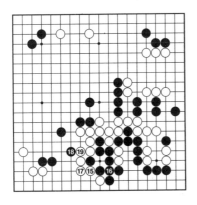
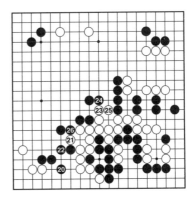

White struggles to live with the sequence to 25, but is left with only one eye when Black plays 26.

Problem 12

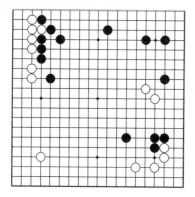 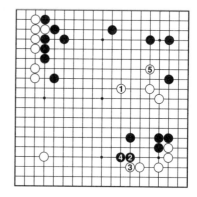

Correct Answer

White should jump lightly out into the center with 1. If Black reinforces the bottom with 2 and 4, White can make good shape in the center with 5.

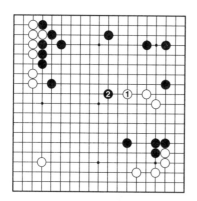 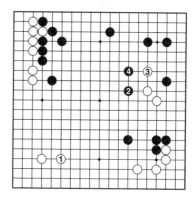

Two White Failures

White 1 in the left diagram is not expansive enough. Black will "cap" with 2. While White struggles to survive, Black will build a large framework of territory at the top left.

In the other diagram, ignoring the right side and reinforcing the lower-left corner with White 1 is a bad strategy since Black will severely attack with 2 and 4. White's stones will survive, but Black has built up a large framework of territory at the top left and solidified the territory at the top.

Problem 13

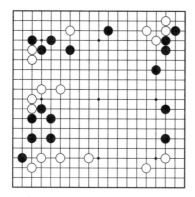 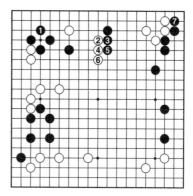

Correct Answer

It is urgent that Black defend the weakness in the upper-left corner by making good shape with 1. To maintain the balance of territory, White has to run away with 2 to 6. However, after making a thick position with 3 and 5, Black can severely attack the white stones in the upper-right corner with 7.

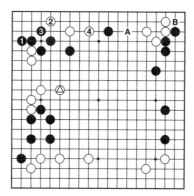

Black's Failure 1

Because White is out in the center with the marked stone, Black 1 is not a severe attack. Therefore, White can ignore it and secure a position at the top with 2 and 4. All of White's stones are now safe, including the ones in the upper-right corner. That is, if Black A, White can secure them with B, and if Black B, White A will attack the black stone at the top.

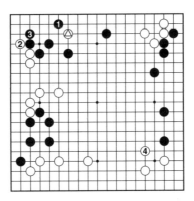

Black's Failure 2

Attacking the marked stone with this Black 1 is not a good move. White forces the exchange of 2 for 3, then reinforces in the lower-right with 4. Black's stones at the top are now over-concentrated.

Problem 14

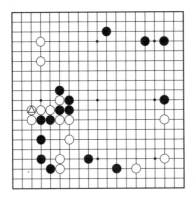

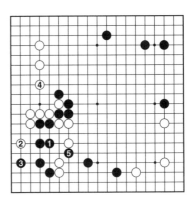

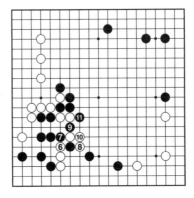

Correct Answer

Black should make shape with 1. If White 2 and 4, then the attachment of 5 is a severe tesuji.

Now White has to block with 6 and save the three stones with 8 and 10, but Black can capture two stones after 11 to make a strong position in the center. White's stones at the lower-left are still not secure and will have to be defended before a play can be made anywhere else.

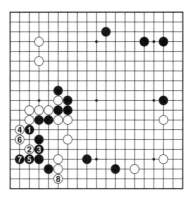

Black's Failure 1

Blocking with 1 leaves Black's stones in the corner thin and vulnerable. White peeps with 2, and Black has no choice but to defend with 3. The sequence to Black 7 is inevitable. Finally, White threatens Black's corner by descending to 8. Black will have to immediately defend, but the two stones to the right have been seriously weakened.

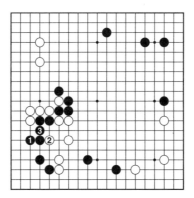

Black's Failure 2

This choice is a better way to defend the corner, but White attaches at the key point of 2, making good shape. Black has to defend with 3, so White can now focus on getting eye shape while attacking the two black stones at the bottom.

Problem 15

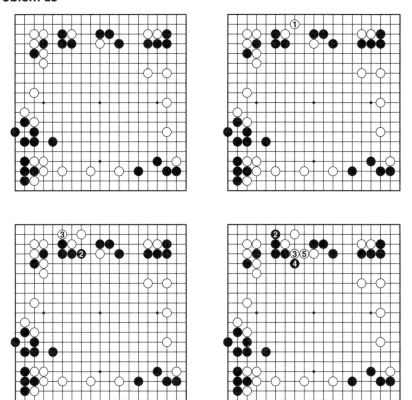

Correct Answer

The diagonal move of 1 is a tesuji that enables White to make sabaki.

There are two possible responses. If Black plays 2, as in the lower-left diagram, White links up at the top with 3.

The other Black 2 prevents the link-up, but White gets out into the center with 3 and 5. There will be a fight with the black group on the left, but White has succeeded in invading the top and will have no trouble connecting up at the bottom or on the right.

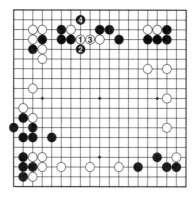

White's Failure

If White omits the tesuji and hanes with 1, after the exchange of Black 2 for White 3, the placement of Black 4 links everything up. Not worried about safety, Black can now focus on attacking White's stones.

Problem 16

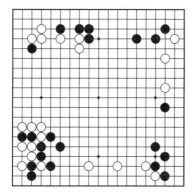
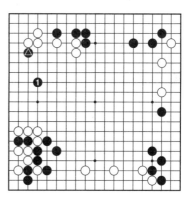

Correct Answer

White has built a large framework of potential territory on the left side so it is urgent that Black invade. Because of the presence of the marked stone, the resulting group will easily live.

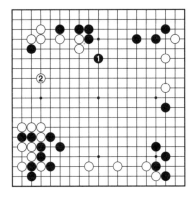

Black's Failure

This Black 1 certainly expands Black's territory at the top, but White 2 reinforces the left side and shifts the balance of territories to White's favor.

Problem 17

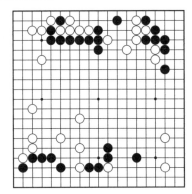
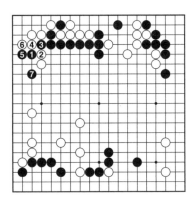

Correct Answer

Black should play the knight's move of 1. If White cuts this stone off with 2 and 4, Black establishes a position with 5 and 7 and should have no problem living since White's two stones are without a base.

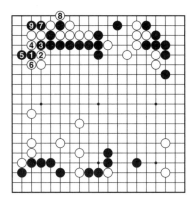

White's Failure

After Black 5, White can't capture the two black stones with 6 because Black ataries with 7, then traps three white stones with 9.

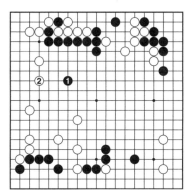

Black's Failure

This Black 1 is a lackluster move. White secures the territory on the left with 2 and Black has lost the chance to wrap up the game.

Problem 18

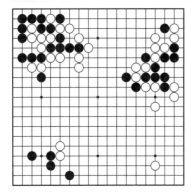 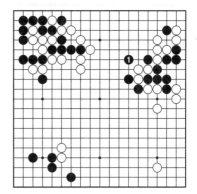

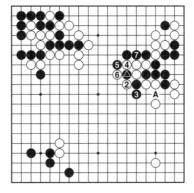

Correct Answer

Jumping ahead of the three white stones with 1 is the tesuji. White's stones can escape with the sequence to 8 (at the marked stone), but Black 3 followed by *A* has ensured the capture of two white stones.

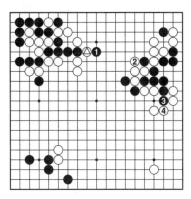

Black's Failure

Trying to set up a ladder by attaching against the marked stone on the left with Black 1 fails. White ataries with 2, and the black stones on the right are trapped. Black 3 leads nowhere, as White simply blocks with 4.

Problem 19

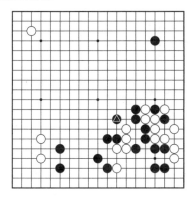 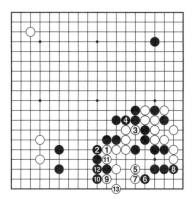

Correct Answer

It is difficult for White to break out into the center, but there are Black weaknesses that can be exploited to make two eyes. If White first pushes with 1, then cuts with 3, Black is forced to respond with 2 and 4. White can now expand the eye space with 5 and 7 while Black has to defend in the corner with 8. Finally, White gets the second eye shape with the sequence to 13.

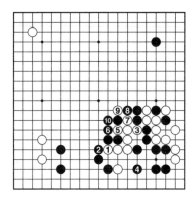 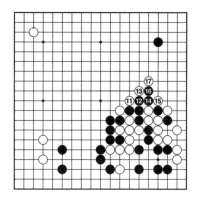

Black's Failure

After White 3, Black 4 is unreasonable. White will push out with 5 and 7, then atari with 9. White can now capture some black stones in a ladder starting with 11.

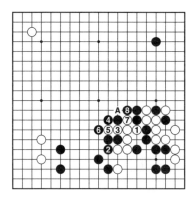

White's Failure

It is the wrong order of moves when White starts by cutting at 1. After Black plays 2, if White tries to push in with 3, 5, and 7, White A is not atari and the white group will die.

Problem 20

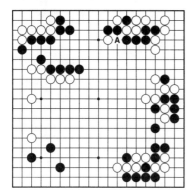 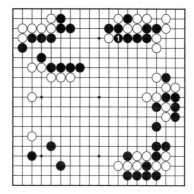

Correct Answer

Black should simply defend against the cut by connecting with 1.

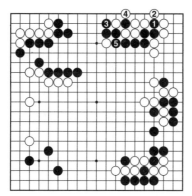

Black's Failure

Most amateurs would want to play 1 and 3 before connecting with 5, believing that they have made some endgame profit. But this is bad style since moves like these should be kept in reserve in case there is a ko and threats are needed.

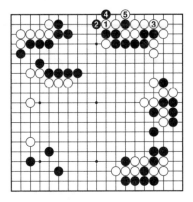
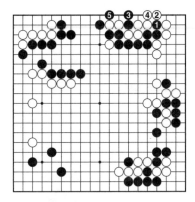

White's Failure

Black's concern is that White will crawl with 1 to gain a couple of endgame points. However, White has to come back and connect at 3, which loses the initiative and allows Black to play the next move elsewhere. Moreover, later on, Black can atari with 4 and force White to take with 5.

White 3 is necessary. If this move is omitted, Black would push in with 1 in the diagram on the right. After White 2, Black can descend to 3. White has no choice but to connect at 4, and this enables Black to capture two stones with 5

Problem 21

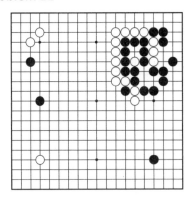
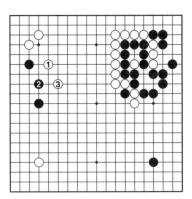

Correct Answer

White has a powerful wall on the right that should be used to attack the black stones on the left with the cap of 1. A vast framework of territory can then be formed at the top with the knight's move of 3.

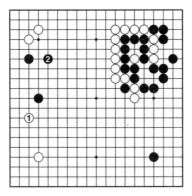

White's Failure 1

Locally, this White 1 is a good move because it attacks Black's thin formation above while mapping out territory in the lower-left. However, Black will jump to 2, neutralizing the influence of White's wall.

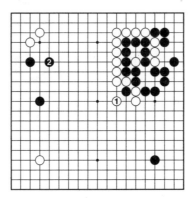

White's Failure 2

Trapping a black stone with White 1 is too small in scale, and is almost beneath consideration. However, many players will make such a move, thinking that it is urgent to secure the two stones that are cut off. In this position though, Black 2 is played at the key point and White loses the initiative.

Problem 22

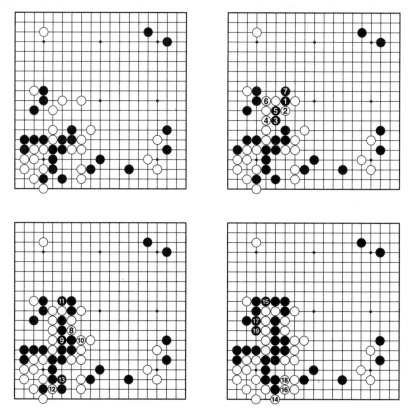

Correct Answer

Wedging in with Black 1 is the tesuji that rescues Black's group. The sequence that follows is forced and Black wins the capturing race by one move.

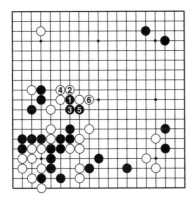 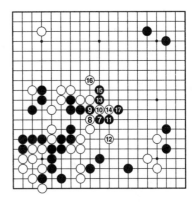

Variation

If White ataries from the outside with 2, Black will play the sequence to 5. After White 6, the knight's move of Black 7 is the tesuji. After Black 11, White can escape with 12, but Black 17 captures two important stones to create a dominating influence on the right side.

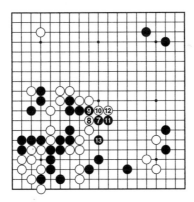

White's Failure

If White tries pressing instead of escaping with 12, Black 13 will kill the group.

Problem 23

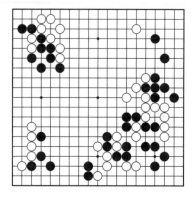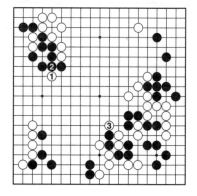

Correct Answer

White should first make a forcing move with 1. If Black connects with 2, White will capture two stones with 3 because 1 has made the ladder favorable for White.

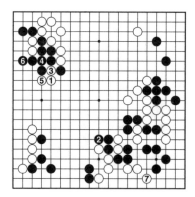

Variation

Suppose that Black ignores White 1 and turns with 2. White will atari with 3, cutting off the marked stone, then turn with 5. Black must answer with 6, so White could make life for the group at the bottom with 7.

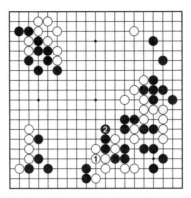

White's Failure

If White tries to get out into the center by connecting with 1, Black will extend to 2. White has lost the initiative.

Problem 24

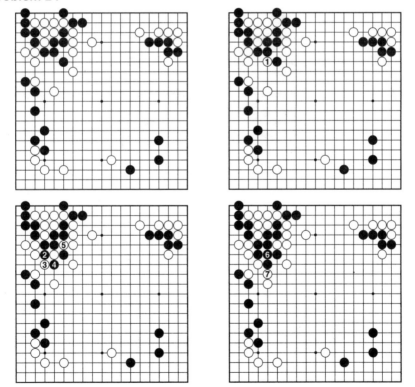

Correct Answer

The tesuji of White 1 is the only move that will enable White to save the corner stones. If Black tries to escape with 2, 4 and 6, White 7 traps the group.

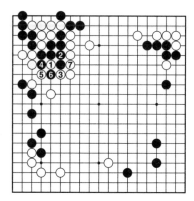

Variation

If Black tries connecting with 2, the sequence to 6 is forced. After White 7, Black is in what is called a "crane's nest" and can't get out of atari by filling in at 1

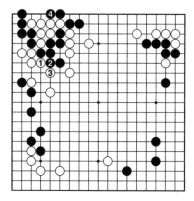

White's failure

This feeble sequence doesn't work since Black 4 leaves White short of liberties.

Suggested Reading

Attack and Defense by Ishida Akira and James Davies
The authors lay down a few clear principles, then go through a wealth of examples and problems from professional play.

The Basics of Go Strategy by Richard Bozulich
The first part is expository, and the second contains 101 problems that expose the reader to various techniques and ways to think about certain kinds of positions.

Get Strong at Invading by Richard Bozulich
There are 171 problems that systematically cover the standard invasions on the side and the corners, attacking corner enclosures and erasing large territorial frameworks.

Get Strong at Attacking by Richard Bozulich
One hundred and thirty-six problems illustrate the various kinds of middle game attacks.

Making Good Shape by Rob van Zeijst and Richard Bozulich
The most thorough review in English of all elements of shape along with several hundred problems.

All About Ko by Rob van Zeijst and Richard Bozulich
The most comprehensive review in any language of all the elements of ko. It also contains 122 problems.

CHAPTER SEVEN

Yose—The Endgame

Three Important Elements of the Endgame

Two fundamental concepts of go are *sente* ("sen-tay") and *gote* ("go-tay"). Simply stated, sente is "Offense"—when one side has the initiative and can move elsewhere after a sequence—while gote is "Defense"—when the opposite is true. Particularly in the endgame, the often complex interplay between these two concepts becomes of paramount importance when the score is close.

The first part of this chapter will demonstrate the four ways gote and sente can interact and the second part and first set of problems will apply these principles to endgame counting.

The last section is devoted to the third important aspect of endgame play—tesuji. As the board situation fills up and becomes more complicated, there is a great temptation for beginners to play unthoughtful, ordinary moves, such as pushing into the opponent's territory or the common place hane-and-connection combinations as shown in Diagrams 2 and 3. Perhaps this is because these are the first endgame moves that one learns. Thus, becoming aware, or more aware, of the tesujis that permeate the diverse shapes of endgame positions will open up a whole new dimension in one's game.

Double Gote

Diagram 1

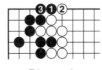

Diagram 2

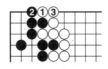

Diagram 3

Diagram 1 shows an endgame position. If Black plays 1 in Diagram 2, White ataries with 2 and Black connects with 3, ending in gote. If White plays 1 in Diagram 3, Black ataries with 2 and White connects with 3, ending in gote. Therefore, whichever side plays first ends in gote.

Double Sente

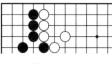

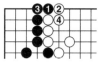
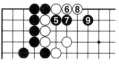

Diagram 4   Diagram 5   Diagram 6

Double sente is a position where the side who plays first ends in sente. Diagram 4 is an example. Suppose that Black plays 1 and 3 in Diagram 5. White must answer with 2 and 4 to defend the territory at the top, so Black ends in sente. If White omits playing 4 in Diagram 5, Black will atari with 5 in Diagram 6. White can't escape with 6 and 8 because Black 9 traps the white stones and White's territory has been decimated. (Instead of playing at 6, White could play at 7 which would preserve more territory, but the loss would still be huge and could also provoke an unwanted ko).

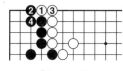
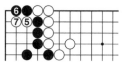

Diagram 7   Diagram 8

On the other hand, if White were to move first with 1 in Diagram 7, Black would end in gote when 4 is played, and White would end in sente. Black can't omit 4 because White would cut with 5 in Diagram 8 and destroy the corner territory.

Being the first to play in a double sente situation is like getting a free move while making a profit. However, the follow-up threat must be big enough to compel an answering move in gote. In other words, as is always the case when playing go, the score and the overall board position must be considered.

One-Sided Sente

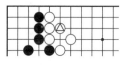
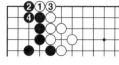
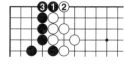

Diagram 9   Diagram 10   Diagram 11

In this kind of endgame position, one side ends in sente while the other side ends in gote. The only difference between Diagram 9 and Diagram 4 is the presence of the marked stone. In Diagram 10, the sequence of White 1 and 3 ends in sente. If Black plays 1 in Diagram 11, Black has to connect at 3 in answer to White 2. However, White no longer needs to make a defensive move because of the marked stone in Diagram 9.

In a one-sided sente situation, the side that ends in sente will usually have the "privilege" of playing first. We say "usually" because of the fourth technique of reverse sente.

Reverse Sente

In a one-sided sente position, the side that would end in gote defends in order to prevent the opponent from making a big sente move.

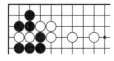
Diagram 12

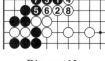
Diagram 13

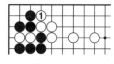
Diagram 14

White's territory at the top in Diagram 12 is open so if Black slides to 1 in Diagram 13, White must answer with 2 and the sequence 8 can be expected. This move is worth seven points and Black can now play elsewhere to gain even more.

However, White can prevent Black from gaining this profit by blocking at 1 in Diagram 14. This kind of endgame move is called reverse sente because it stops Black from making a sente move worth seven points. Therefore, White should play 1 when all other sente moves on the board are worth less.

Values of Endgame Moves

Example 1

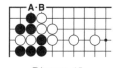
Diagram 15

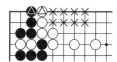
Diagram 16

After White plays 1 in Diagram 14, Black and White will each have a 50% chance to play the small endgame moves at *A* or *B* in Diagram 15. This is because with small endgame moves, whatever points would be gained and lost will be compensated for in other areas of the board, Thus, for the purpose of calculation, we assume that White and Black played the triangled stones in Diagram 16

Therefore, by playing 1 in Diagram 13, Black deprived White of the six *X*-marked points in Diagram 16 and gained the point where the marked stone is now located.

Considering the situation from White's point of view, by playing 1 in Diagram 14, White has gained the six *X*-marked points in Diagram 16 and deprived Black of the point where the marked stone is located.

Hence, Black 1 in Diagram 13 is worth about seven points in sente, while White 1 in Diagram 14 is worth about seven points in reverse sente.

We say "about" because the overall situation, such as the value of follow-up moves, the presence of ko and possible changes of strategies have to be considered. Nevertheless, to roughly calculate the value of sente and gote, go players traditionally divide by two the value of gote moves, give full value to sente and reverse-sente moves and double the value of double-sente moves. However, in the problem section that follows, we will assume that the rest of the game is uncomplicated.

Example 2

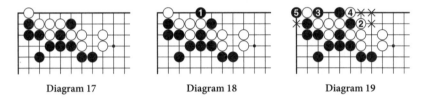

Diagram 17   Diagram 18   Diagram 19

The hane of Black 1 in Diagram 18 is a tesuji. In Diagram 19, White can capture two stones with 2 and 4 and Black captures a stone with 3 and 5 in gote.

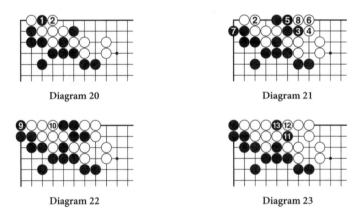

Diagram 20   Diagram 21

Diagram 22   Diagram 23

Throwing in a stone with Black 1 in Diagram 20 might seem like a tesuji, but, after White captures with 2, Black has no follow-up and gets two points less territory than in Diagram 19.

What happens if White resists by connecting with 2 in Diagram 21? Black will play 3 and 5, then force White to capture with 7 and 9. Next, Black ataries with 11 in Diagram 22 and captures seven stones with 13.

In Diagram 19, White got the three points marked *X* and captured the marked stone and the stone at 1 in Diagram 18 for a total of seven points. Black captured the marked stone and has taken the point *X* for a total of two points. This is a difference of five points in White's favor.

In 23, after filling in at the marked stone, Black took seven stones and gained six points of territory, while White only captured four stones, so there is a difference of nine points in Black's favor. Resistance has led to a huge loss for White.

Example 3

There is a useful method for quickly calculating the gains and losses involved in who plays first.

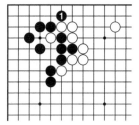

Diagram 24

How many points is Black 1 worth?

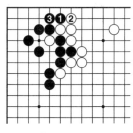

Diagram 25

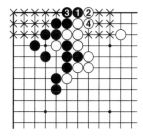

Diagram 26

After Black 1, the exchange of White 2 for Black 3 in gote can be expected. Black 1 and 3 in Diagram 25 are now Black's privilege since White 4 would end the sequence in gote. Black would get 12 points (the *X*-marked points on the left) and White would get seven points (the *X*-marked points on the right).

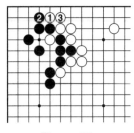

Diagram 27

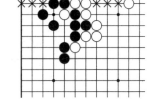

Diagram 28

If White were to play first, 1 and 3 would end in gote but White 1 and 3 in Diagram 28 are now White's privilege, so Black ends in gote and gets seven points, while White gets 12.

Black would get 12 points of territory in Diagram 26 and seven points in Diagram 28, a difference of five points. White would get seven points of territory in Diagram 26 and 12 points in Diagram 28 for a difference of five points. Adding these differences, Black 1 in Diagram 24 would be worth ten points in gote.

The reader will notice that as long as the initial X's exceed the territories won and lost, their amount is irrelevant and only provide a handy basis for comparisons.

The following problems will further explore the intricacies of the endgame.

Endgame Counting Problems

What are the values of Black's moves?

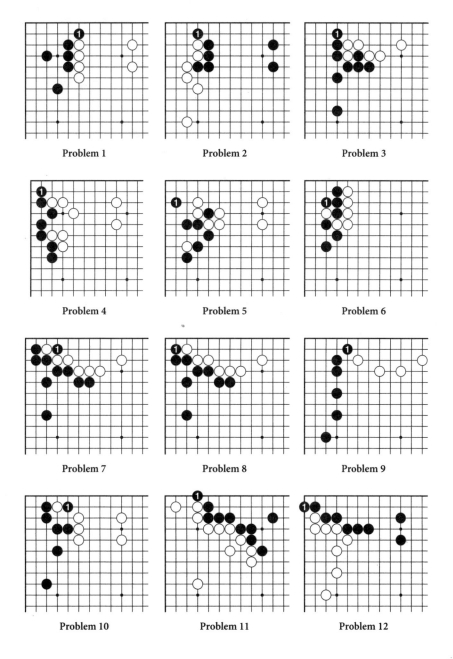

Problem 1

Problem 2

Problem 3

Problem 4

Problem 5

Problem 6

Problem 7

Problem 8

Problem 9

Problem 10

Problem 11

Problem 12

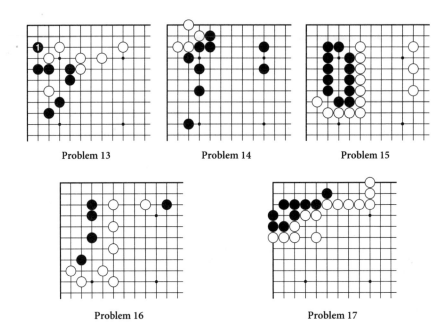

Problem 13   Problem 14   Problem 15

Problem 16   Problem 17

Answers to the Endgame Counting Problems

Problem 1

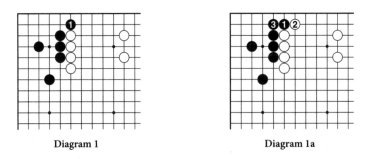

Diagram 1   Diagram 1a

14 Points in Gote

After Black 1, the exchange of White 2 for Black 3 can be expected. Black ends in gote.

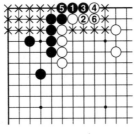

Diagram 1b

Black's Privilege

Black 1 and 3 are now Black's privilege. White 4 ends in gote. Black gets 13 points and White gets six.

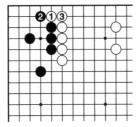

Diagram 1c

If White Plays First

If White were to play first, the sequence to White 3 ends in gote.

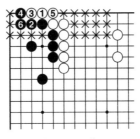

Diagram 1d

White's Privilege

White 1 and 3 are now White's privilege and Black 6 ends in gote. Black gets six points and White gets 13.

Black got 13 points of territory in Diagram 1a and six points in Diagram 1c, a difference of seven points. White got six points of territory in Diagram 1a and 13 points in Diagram 1c, a difference of seven points. The total is 14 points in gote.

Problem 2

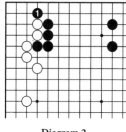
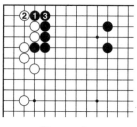

Diagram 2   Diagram 2a

17 Points in Gote

After Black 1, the exchange of White 2 for Black 3 ends in gote.

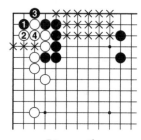

Diagram 2b

Black's Privilege

Black 1 and 3 are now Black's privilege and White 4 ends in gote. Black gets 16 points and White gets three.

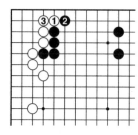

Diagram 2c

If White Plays First

If White were to play first the sequence to White 3 would end in gote.

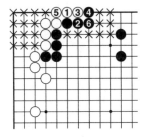

Diagram 2d

White's Privilege

White 1 to 5 in Diagram 2d are now White's privilege. Black 6 ends in gote. Black gets nine points and White gets 13 points.

Black got 16 points of territory in Diagram 2c and nine points in Diagram 2d, a difference of seven points. White got three points of territory in Diagram 2b and 13 points in Diagram 2d, for a difference of ten points. Adding this difference, Black 1 in the problem diagram is worth 17 points in gote.

Problem 3

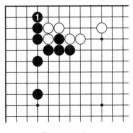

Diagram 3

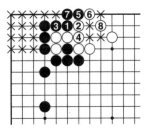

Diagram 3a

19 Points in Gote

After Black 1 in the problem diagram, Black 1 and 3 are Black's privilege and White 8 ends in gote. Black gets 14 points and White gets four points.

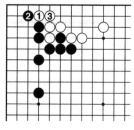

Diagram 3b

If White Plays First

If White were to play first, the sequence to White 3 would end in gote.

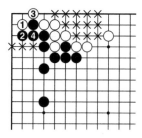

Diagram 3c

White's Privilege

White 1 and 3 are now White's privilege with Black 4 ending in gote. Black would get three points and White would get 12.

Black got 14 points in Diagram 3a and three points in Diagram 3d, a difference of 11 points. White got four points in Diagram 3a and 12 points in Diagram 3c, an eight-point difference.

Adding this difference, Black 1 in the problem diagram is worth 19 points in gote.

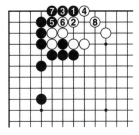

Diagram 3d

The Monkey Jump

Beginners might be tempted to try the "monkey jump" of Black 1 but this is worth two points less than the results in Diagram 3a.

Problem 4

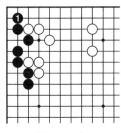

Diagram 4

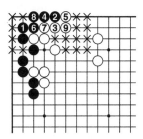

Diagram 4a

11 Points in Gote

After Black's move in the problem diagram, Black 1 to 8 are Black's privilege with White 9 ending in gote. Black gets six points and White gets 11.

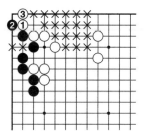

Diagram 4b

If White Plays First

If White were to play 1 and 3 in Diagram 4b, it would end in gote. Black gets two points and White gets 18. Black got six points of territory in Diagram 4a and two points in Diagram 4b, for a four-point difference. White got 11 points of territory in Diagram 4a and 18 points in Diagram 4b for a seven-point difference. Adding this difference, we can conclude that Black 1 in the problem diagram is worth 11 points in gote.

Problem 5

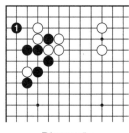

Diagram 5

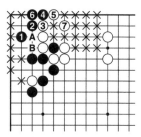

Diagram 5a

20 Points in Gote

After Black 1 in the problem diagram, Black 2 to 5 in Diagram 5a are Black's privilege. White 6 ends in gote. Black gets nine points and White gets 16 points with the added privilege of playing A and B.

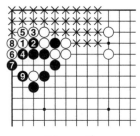

Diagram 5b

If White Plays First

If White were to play first, the sequence from 1 to 5 ends in gote. Later, 7 and 9 are White's privilege. Black gets zero points and White gets 27. Black got nine points of territory in Diagram 5a and zero points in Diagram 5b for a difference of nine points.

White got 16 points of territory in Diagram 5a and 27 points in Diagram 5b, a difference of 11 points. Adding these differences indicates that Black 1 in the problem diagram is worth 20 points in gote.

Problem 6

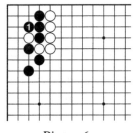

Diagram 6

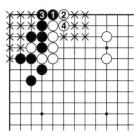

Diagram 6a

11 Points in Gote

After Black 1 in the problem diagram, Black 1 and 3 are Black's privilege with White 4 ending in gote. Black gets 11 points and White gets 7.

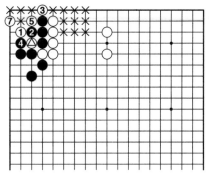

Diagram 6b

If White Plays First

If White were to play first, the sequence to 7 (with Black filling at 6) would end in gote. White gets 14 points of territory and Black is left with only one point for capturing the marked stone. Black got 11 points of territory in Diagram 6a and one point in Diagram 6b for a ten-point difference. White got seven points of territory in Diagram 6a and 14 points in Diagram 6b, a seven-point difference. Adding these together, we find that Black 1 in the problem diagram is worth 18 points in gote.

Problem 7

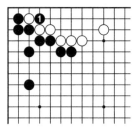

Diagram 7

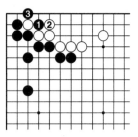

Diagram 7a

Ten Points in Gote

After Black 1, White will exchange 2 for Black 3.

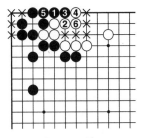

Diagram 7b

Black's Privilege

Black 1 and 3 are Black's privilege and with 6, White ends in gote. Black has captured a stone at *A* (two points) and gets the four points on the left for a total of six. White gets the five points on the right.

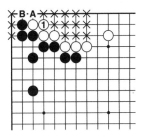

Diagram 7c

If White Plays First

White would connect at 1. Later, there is almost the same chance that Black will play *A* or White will play *B*, so we assume the exchange of White *A* for Black *B*.

Black got six points of territory in Diagram 7c and three points in Diagram 7c for a three-point difference. White got five points of territory in Diagram 7b and 12 points in Diagram 7c for a seven-point difference. Adding the differences indicates that Black 1 in the problem diagram is worth ten points in gote.

Problem 8

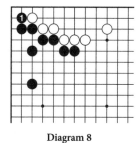

Diagram 8

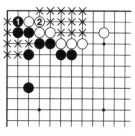

Diagram 8a

14 Points in Gote

If the game is down to five point gote moves, there is a 50% chance that White will Answer Black 1 by connecting in gote with 2 ...

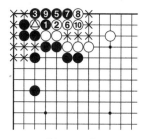

Diagram 8b

White Plays Elsewhere

... however, it is just as likely that White will play elsewhere and allow Black to capture with 1 and 3. Black ends in gote, but has the privilege to play the sequence 9 in sente.

We saw that the difference between Diagram 7a and 7b in Problem 27 is ten points in gote. However, since the chances of White 2 in Diagram 8a or Black 1 in Diagram 8b are even, we give the value of White 1 in Diagram 8a or Black 1 in Diagram 8b as five points.

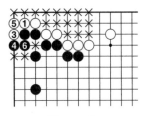

Diagram 8c

If White Plays First

Instead of Black 1 in the problem diagram, suppose White played at 1. It would then be White's privilege to play 3 and 5 in sente. In this position, White would get 16 points of territory and Black gets three points. The difference between Diagram 8a where Black got eight points and White got 12, and Diagram 8c where Black got three and White 16 would be nine points. However, since there is a 50% chance that White will play 1 in Diagram 8a or Black will play 1 in Diagram 8b, we must add five points, giving a value of 14 points in gote for Black 1 in the problem diagram.

Problem 9

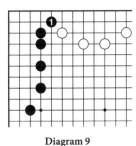

Diagram 9   Diagram 9a

6 Points in Double Sente

In answer to Black 1, White must defend the territory at the top with 2. Black can continue with 3 and 5, so White must connect at 6, ending in gote. The exchange of White A for Black B is White's privilege. Black gets ten points and White gets seven.

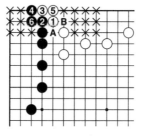

Diagram 9b

If White Played First

If White played first, the sequence to five ends in sente and the exchange of White *A* for Black *B* is White's privilege. White gets ten points of territory and Black gets seven. Black got ten points of territory in Diagram 9a and seven points in Diagram 9b, a three-point difference. White got seven points of territory in Diagram 9a and ten points in Diagram 9b, a three-point difference.

By adding these, we conclude that Black 1 in the problem diagram is worth six points in double sente.

Problem 10

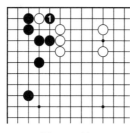

Diagram 10

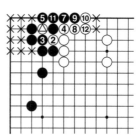

Diagram 10a

12 Points in Gote

Black can capture the marked stone in gote with the sequence to 5. Later, the sequence to White 12 is Black's privilege. Black gets 12 points (the ten *X*-marked points on the left plus two points for capturing the marked stone). White gets the two points at the top.

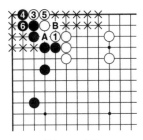

Diagram 10b

If White Plays First

White would play 1 in gote and then could play 3 and 5 in sente. Black gets seven points on the left and White gets nine points at the top, leaving Black *A* for White *B* as Black's privilege.

Black got 12 points of territory in Diagram 10a and seven points in Diagram 10b, a five-point difference. White got two points of territory in Diagram 10a and nine points in Diagram 10b, a seven-point difference. Adding this difference, we can conclude that Black 1 in Diagram 10a is worth 12 points in gote.

Problem 11

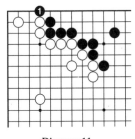

Diagram 11

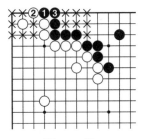

Diagram 11a

Three Points in Reverse Sente

Black plays 1 and ends in gote after the exchange of White 2 for 3. White gets seven points on the left, and Black gets seven at the top.

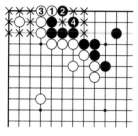

Diagram 11b

If White Plays First

If White played 1 and 3, it would be in sente since Black would have to defend with 4 in gote. Black gets five points and White gets eight.

Black got seven points of territory in Diagram 11a and five points in Diagram 11b for a two point difference. White got seven points of territory in Diagram 11a and eight points in Diagram 11b for a difference of one point. Adding it up, Black 1 in Diagram 11a is worth three points.

Since it is gote for Black to play 1 in Diagram 11a and sente for White to play 1 in Diagram 11b , this is a one-sided sente situation. Therefore, Black 1 is worth three points in reverse sente.

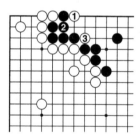

Diagram 11c

Black Plays Elsewhere

After White 3 in Diagram 11b , Black has to defend with 4. If 4 is played else-where, White will atari with 1. Black cannot connect with 2 because White would atari with 3.

Problem 12

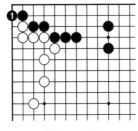

Diagram 12

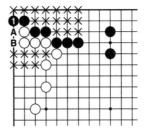

Diagram 12a

Four Points in Reverse Sente

After 1, Black ends in gote. Later, the exchange of A for White B is Black's privilege. White gets the seven points on the left, and Black gets 15 points at the top.

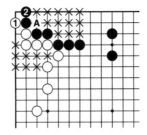

Diagram 12b

If White Plays First

White 1 is sente since Black has to descend to 2 and eventually must connect at A. White gets eight points and Black gets 12.

White got seven points of territory in Diagram 12a and eight points in Diagram 12b, a one-point difference. Black got 15 points of territory in Diagram 12a and 12 points in Diagram 12b, a three-point difference. Adding these together indicates that Black 1 in Diagram 12a is worth four points.

As in Problem 11, since it is gote for Black to play 1 in Diagram 12a and sente for White to play 1 in Diagram 12b, this is a one-sided sente situation. Therefore, Black 1 is worth four points in reverse sente.

Problem 13

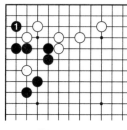

Diagram 13

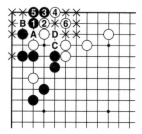

Diagram 13a

16 Points in Gote

After Black plays the marked stone, the sequence to 5 is Black's privilege. Exchanging A for Black B is White's privilege, and exchanging C for White D is Black's privilege. When the position finally settles down, Black would get five points and White six.

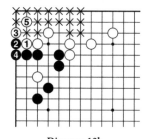

Diagram 13b

If White Plays First

After White 1, Black can play 2 and 4 in sente. White gets the 17 points at the top and Black gets zero.

White got six points of territory in Diagram 13a and 17 points in Diagram 13b, an 11-point difference. Black got five points of territory in Diagram 13a and zero points in Diagram 13b for a 5-point difference. By adding the differences, the conclusion is that Black 1 in Diagram 13a is worth 16 points in gote.

Problem 14

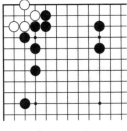

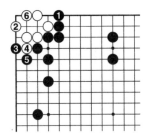

Diagram 14   Diagram 14a

Correct Answer

Black should first descend to 1, forcing White to defend the corner with 2. Next, jumping down to the first line with 3 is a tesuji. After exchanging 4 for Black 5, White can reduce Black's territory on the left by only one point.

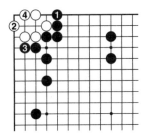

Diagram 14b

Black's Failure

After White defends with 2, Black 3 is a mistake.

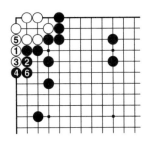

Diagram 14c

Continuation

Later, it is White's privilege to play the sequence to 5 in sente. Black's territory in this diagram is two points less than in Diagram 14a.

Problem 15

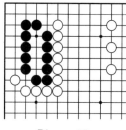 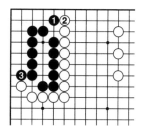

Diagram 15   Diagam 15a

Correct Answer

Black should play 1. This move threatens to lay waste to a large White territory on the right, so White must block with 2. Black can now defend the territory on the left with 3.

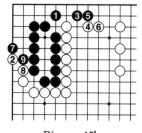

Diagram 15b

White's Failure

If White reduces Black's territory on the left with 2, Black jumps to 3 and pushes once with 5. After a gote White 6, Black defends the left with 7 and 9.

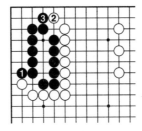

Diagram 15c

Black's Failure

If Black meekly defends with 1, White plays the second move in sente with 2.

Problem 16

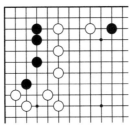

Diagram 16

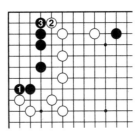

Diagram 16a

Correct Answer

In this case, White is threatening to invade a large black territory, so Black should defend with 1, even though White can follow up with another endgame move at 2.

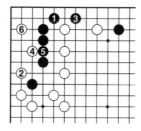

Diagram 16b

Black's Failure

If Black ignores White's threat (the marked stone in the problem diagram) and plays 1, White will jump into black territory with 2. Black 3 does not deprive White of much territory, but White 4 and 6 wipe out all the remaining territory in the corner.

Problem 17

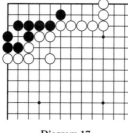

Diagram 17

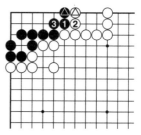

Diagram 17a

Six Points in Gote

After Black 1, the exchange of White 2 for Black 3 can be expected. Black ends in gote. There is a 50% chance that Black will play on the marked white stone or White will play on the marked black stone, so, for the purpose of calculation, we can assume White and Black have played the triangled stones. Counting the territories, we see that Black has 11 points and White has four points.

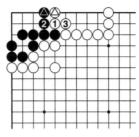

Diagram 17b

If White Plays First

If White were to play first, the sequence to 3 ends in gote. Counting the territories, we see that Black has eight points and White has seven points. Black got 11 points of territory in Diagram 17a, but only eight points in Diagram 17b for a difference of three points. White got four points in Diagram 17a, but seven points in Diagram 17b. Again, there is a difference of three points. Adding this difference, we can conclude that Black 1 in the problem diagram is worth six points in gote.

Endgame Tesuji Problems

Black to Play

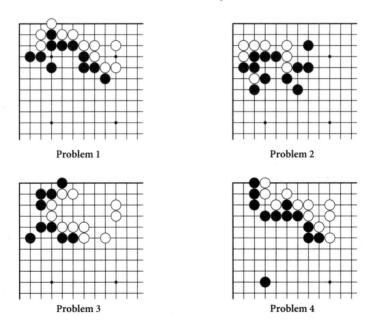

Problem 1

Problem 2

Problem 3

Problem 4

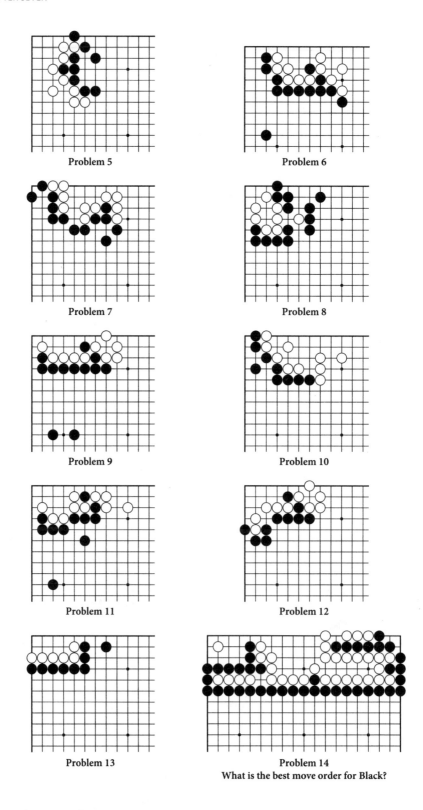

Problem 5

Problem 6

Problem 7

Problem 8

Problem 9

Problem 10

Problem 11

Problem 12

Problem 13

Problem 14
What is the best move order for Black?

Answers to Endgame Tesuji Problems

Problem 1

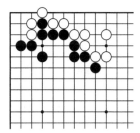 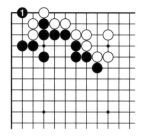

Correct Answer

The peep of Black 1 is the tesuji.

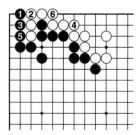

Continuation

White must connect with 2. After this, the sequence to 6 is forced and White ends in gote.

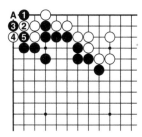

White's Failure

After Black 1, White can resist with 2 and 4. The result is a ko after Black 5 and White A taking 3, but Black is happy to fight this ko because White has more to lose.

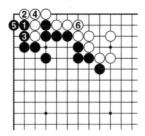

Black's Failure

The attachment of White 1 is a lackluster move. White will hane while 2 and the sequence to White 6 can now be expected. Compared with the correct answer, Black has lost the point at 5 and the point above 5.

Problem 2

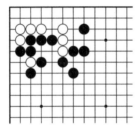
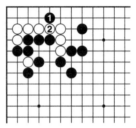

Correct Answer

The placement of Black 1 is the tesuji. White must connect with 2 …

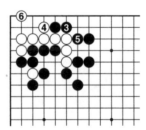

Continuation

… while Black links up with 3 and 5. White must live in gote with 6.

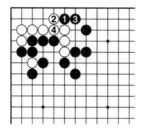

Black's Failure 1

Black 1 may look like a tesuji, but White lives with 2 and 4 and ends up with three more points than in the continuation diagram.

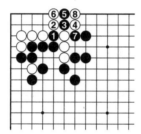

Black's Failure 2

Black 1 is simply clumsy and White connects up with little effort.

Problem 3

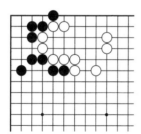
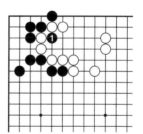

Correct Answer

The cut of Black 1 is the tesuji.

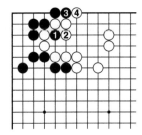

Continuation

White 2 is the best response. The sequence is forced …

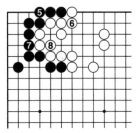

Continuation

… and White must capture with 8 in gote.

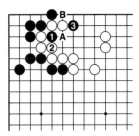

White's Failure

If White connects with 2, Black 3 lays waste to White's territory. If White captures at *A*, Black links up at *B* and if White *B*, then Black *A*.

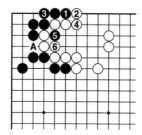

Black's Failure

Simply playing Black 1 and 3 are dull moves. After White 4, Black 5 is ineffective. Moreover, *A* now becomes White's privilege. Compared to the correct answer, this is a difference of two points in favor of White.

Problem 4

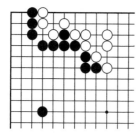
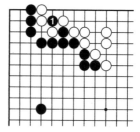

Correct Answer

A throw-in is the tesuji.

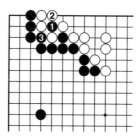

Continuation

White must capture with 2 and Black ataries with 3.

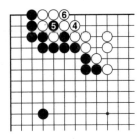

Continuation

Next, White must connect with 4 to avoid a further loss. Finally, Black takes the ko with 5. This is a flower-viewing ko, so White can't afford to fight it and must humbly connect with 6.

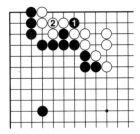

Black's Failure

If Black cuts with 1, White will connect at the vital point of 2, and Black has no follow-up.

Problem 5

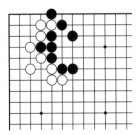   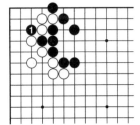

Correct Answer

The cut of Black 1 is the tesuji.

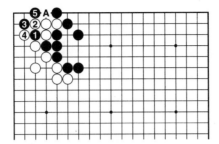

Continuation

If White ataries with 2, Black hanes with 3, letting White capture a stone with 4. Next, Black plays 5 and has successfully encroached upon White's corner territory. Note that White can't play at A because of a shortage of liberties.

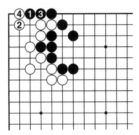

Black's Failure 1

Black can make some inroads into White's corner with the placement of 1, but White still gets a sizeable corner with 2 and 4. This result is better for White than the one in the correct answer diagram.

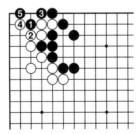

Black's Failure 2

The attachment of Black 1 leads to a ko. The correct answer is clearly better for Black.

Problem 6

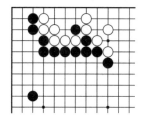 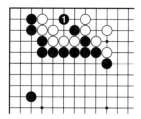

Correct Answer

The diagonal move of Black 1 is the tesuji.

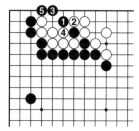

Continuation

When White ataries with 2, Black plays another diagonal move with 3. White must capture with 4 and Black links up with 5.

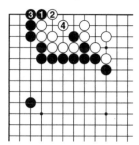

Black's failure

Black 1 and 3 are ordinary endgame moves. The result here is at least six points better for White than the correct answer.

Problem 7

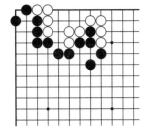
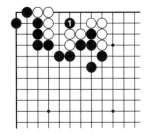

Correct Answer

The attachment of Black 1 is the tesuji.

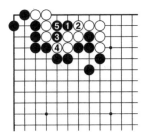

Continuation

White's best response is to connect with 2. After the sequence to 5, White loses four stones.

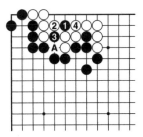

White's Failure 1

If White plays 2, Black ataries with 3 and White has no choice but to connect with 4. Black will now capture five stones instead of four stones in the continuation. Note that if White captures at *A*, Black ataries at 4 and there is no escape.

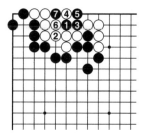

White's Failure 2

White could also connect with 2 and this leads to a ko when Black captures with 7. If Black wins this ko, White's loss would be much bigger than in the continuation. Moreover, this is a "flower-viewing" ko, as the Japanese call it, meaning Black risks nothing.

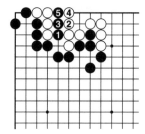

Black's Failure

Rather than playing the correct move, Black can also capture four white stones by wedging in with 1, but White then ends up with two more points of territory.

Problem 8

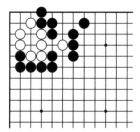
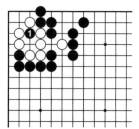

Correct Answer

Throwing in a stone is the tesuji.

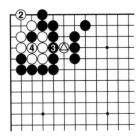

Continuation

White must now play 2 to get two eyes. Black then ataries with 3 and captures the marked stone in sente.

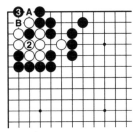

White's Failure 1

If White captures with 2, Black will play 3, and White can't get two eyes. That is, if White blocks at *A*, Black will atari at *B*.

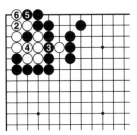

White's Failure 2

If White plays 2, the sequence to White 6 results in one point less than if the correct move was made.

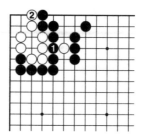

Black's Failure

Instead of playing the correct move, if Black simply connects at 1, White ends up with seven points of territory instead of six points.

Problem 9

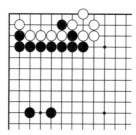
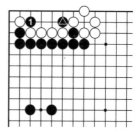

Correct Answer

Cutting with Black 1 is the tesuji.

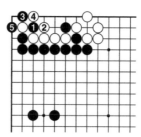

Continuation

White 2 and 4 are the proper responses. After Black 5, the position is a two-stage ko, meaning that White must win twice to salvage the corner. Playing where the opponent wants to (or should) play is often good advice. In this case, at the end of a long and complicated joseki, White should have protected the corner because of the marked cutting stone in the correct answer diagram.

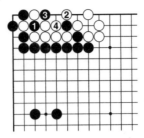

White's Failure

If White plays elsewhere after Black 5 in the above diagram, taking the ko with 1 is severe. If there are not enough ko threats, White will have to fall back and capture a black stone with 2 and 4. Black has made a big profit in the corner.

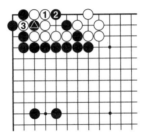

White's Failure 2

In answer to the marked stone, White might consider playing at 1. Black will play 2, and the stakes for White have been raised enormously since it is a flower-viewing ko for Black.

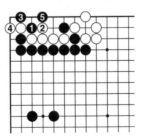

White's Failure 3

Instead of 4 in the correct answer diagram, White might resist by descending to this 4 on the left. However, it also becomes a flower-viewing ko when Black ataries with 5. White can't play this way either.

Problem 10

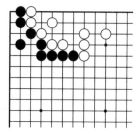 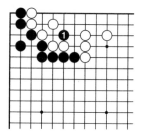

White's Failure

The attachment of Black 1 is the tesuji.

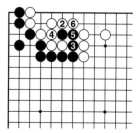

Continuation

White 2 is the best response. In the sequence to White 6, Black ends in sente and has made inroads into White's territory.

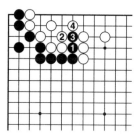

Black's Failure

Instead of starting correctly, if Black pushes in with 1, White falls back with 2. Black continues with 3, but now White blocks with 4. This result is two points better for White.

Problem 11

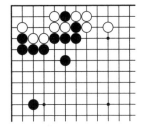 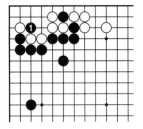

Correct Answer

The cut of Black 1 is the tesuji.

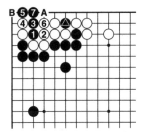

Continuation

If White ataries with 2, the sequence to Black 7 can be expected. However, Black cannot be captured because White can't play at *A* until after the marked stone is taken and can't play at *B* without being captured. Therefore, Black can take the two white stones on the left.

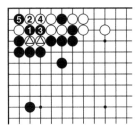

Variation

White might resist with 2, sacrificing the two marked stones. However, the result here is the same.

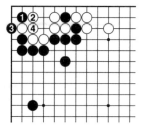

Black's Failure 1

The clamp of Black 1 is a tesuji often seen in this kind of position. However, in this case it is not as effective as the correct moves.

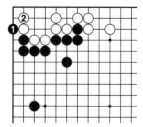

Black's failure 2

Black 1 is a lackluster move. White simply extends to 2 and takes a sizeable profit at the top.

Problem 12

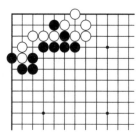

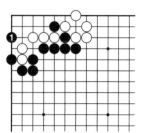

Correct Answer

The placement of Black 1 is the tesuji.

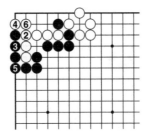

Continuation

White has no choice but to connect with 2. With the sequence to 6, Black has reduced White's corner territory and ends in sente.

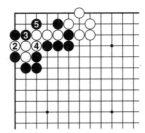

White's Mistake

Wedging in with 2 is a mistake. Black ataries with 3 and 5 and captures seven stones. Instead of 4, White has to limit the loss by playing 4 above 3 and connecting with 5.

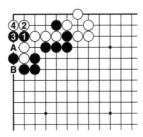

Black's Failure 1

If Black plays 1, White ataries with 2 and 4. Now Black can't connect at *A* because of a liberty shortage. If Black connects at *B*, White captures two stones with *A*.

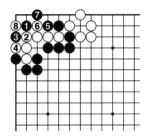

Black's Failure 2

The placement of Black 1 also fails. White connects with 2, and secures the entire corner with the sequence to 8.

Problem 13

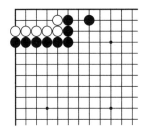 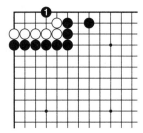

Correct Answer

The placement of Black 1 is the tesuji.

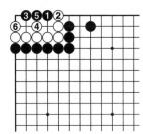

Continuation

White must block with 2. Next, Black jumps to 3, and the sequence to White 6 is forced. White's stones are alive in a seki, so White gets no points.

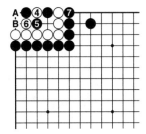

Variation

After Black 3 in the correct answer diagram, White could resist by throwing in a stone with 4 and Black would capture with 5. After White 6, Black fills a liberty with 7. White can now start a ko by throwing in a stone at *A*. On the other hand, Black could also start one by throwing in a stone at *B*. Whichever side starts the ko gives the other side the first capture, so Black should wait to let White begin. Once White starts, it becomes a flower-viewing ko, so Black would have nothing to lose.

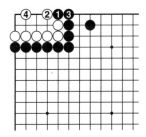

Black's Failure

Black 1 and 3 are ordinary endgame moves. After 3, White lives in the corner with 4 and gets six points of territory.

Problem 14

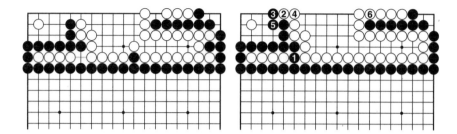

Failure

At first glance, capturing four stones with Black 1 looks like the "biggest move." It is worth eight points, however, it is in gote, while White gets to play 2 and 4 in sente. Black must connect with 5 so White rescues the three stones on the right with 6.

Black has a total of 22 points with 11 points in the upper-left corner, three points in the upper-right corner, plus eight points for the four stones that were captured with 5. White has a total of 22 points with five points on the right plus 17 points in the middle of the top, so this game is a draw or, as it is called in Japanese, a *jigo* ("gee-go").

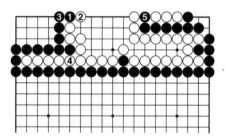

Correct Answer

Black must first play the "smallest move" of 1 and 3 which is worth only two points in gote, but it is actually the biggest move. Next, White plays the "biggest" move by connecting with 4 and saving four stones which is worth eight points in gote. Black then takes three stones worth six points in gote with the remaining move.

Counting the territories, Black has a total of 22 points, with 13 points in the upper-left corner, three points in the upper-right, plus six points for the three stones that were captured with 5. With five points on the right plus 16 points in the middle of the top, White has 21 points so Black wins by one point.

Miai

The lesson to be drawn from this "counting tesuji" is that if there are two gote moves of equal or almost equal value at any point in the game, they will cancel each other out, so it is more profitable to play another move that does not have an equivalent counterpart. This principle is known as *"miai"* ("me-eye") in Japanese.

Suggested Reading

The Endgame by Ogawa Tomoko 6-dan and James Davies

This book covers everything from basic counting and endgame tesuji to the macro-endgame.

Get Strong at the Endgame by Richard Bozulich

A complete book on the endgame with tesuji, calculation problems, tests and game positions.

Explanations and Pronunciations of Japanese Terms Used in this Book

Aji (*"ah-gee"*) p. 27

Atari (*"ah-tar-ee"*) p. 9

Fuseki (*"foo-se-key"*)" p. 17

Gote (*"go-tay"*) p. 205

Hane (*"han-nay"*) p. 14

Jigo (*"gee-go"*) p. 254

Joseki (*"joe-se-key"*) p. 11

Ko (*"koh"*) p. 10

Miai (*"me-eye"*) p. 255

Ponnuki (*"pon-new-key"*) p. 10

Sabaki (*"sa-bak-kee"*) p. 14

Seki (*"se-key"*) p. 70

Sente (*"sen-tay"*) p. 205